MW00713036

SRA Art Connections

Level 5

Authors

Rosalind Ragans, Ph.D., Senior Author

Willis Bing Davis
Tina Farrell
Jane Rhoades Hudak, Ph.D.
Gloria McCoy
Bunyan Morris
Nan Yoshida

Contributing Writers

Dennis Black
Jackie Ellett

Education Division
Performing Arts Center of Los Angeles County

Columbus, Ohio

A Division of The McGraw·Hill Companies

Credits

Cover, Katsushika Hokusai, *The Great Wave off Kanagawa*, The Metropolitan Museum of Art, New York, NY. H.O. Havemeyer Collection, Bequest of Mrs. H. O. Havemeyer, 1929; **Back Cover**, top Dustin Sandidge, Age 11, *Night City,* middle Tiffany Hayes, Age 9, *The Encounter,* bottom Robert Landers, Age 11, *Rainbow over the Mountains*; **15**, Photo courtesy of the Steinbaum Krauss Gallery; **40**, Photo by Craig Schwartz ©1990; **43**, Photograph courtesy of Marsha Jessup; **45**, *Claude Monet seated beside the water lily pond at Giverny* ©Archive Photos, New York, NY; **70**, Courtesy of Rhapsody in Taps. Photo by Phillip Channing; **73**, Photograph courtesy of Richard Tichich; **75**, Erich Lessing/Art Resource, NY; **86**, left ©Dennis M. Gottlieb/The Stock Market; ©Donald Johnston/Tony Stone Images; **98**, top left ©Christine L. Coscioni; top right ©PhotoDisc; bottom right ©Christine L. Coscioni; bottom left ©Christine L. Coscioni; **100**, Photo by Silvia Mautner; **103**, Photograph courtesy of National Gallery of Art, Washington, DC; **105**, Albright-Knox Art Gallery, Buffalo, NY. Bequest of A. Conger Goodyear, 1966; **130**, Photo by Craig Schwartz ©1993; **133**, Photograph courtesy of The Metropolitan Museum of Art, New York, NY; **135**, Henri Cartier-Bresson/Magnum Photos; **146**, top ©Zanetti/The Stock Market; ©David S. Waitz; **160**, Photo courtesy of Ballet Folklorico de Mexico; **163**, Photograph ©1996, The Art Institute of Chicago, Photograph by Thomas Cinoman; **165**, Ap/Wide World Photos; **190**, Photo by Craig Schwartz ©1993; **193**, Photograph courtesy of Iris Sandkühler; **214**, *Adena Effigy Figure (Adena Pipe)*, Courtesy of the Ohio Historical Society; *Three Cows and One Horse, ceiling of the Axial Gallery, Lascaux Caves in France*, ©Douglas Mazonowicz/Gallery of Prehistoric Art; *Statues from Abu Temple*, Courtesy of The Oriental Institute of The University of Chicago, Photograph by Victor J. Boswell; *Tutankhamen Mask (Side View)*, ©Brian Brake, Photo Researchers; *Kuang (Gong with Lid)*, Asian Art Museum of San Francisco, The Avery Brundage Collection; **215**, *Colossal Head*, La Venta, Mexico, ©Nathaniel Tarn, Photo Researchers; *Woman Playing Harp*, ©1989 The Metropolitan Museum of Art, NY, Fletcher Fund, 1956, (56.171.38); *Stonehenge*, ©1984 Lawrence Migdale/Photo Researchers, Inc.; *Parthenon*, ©Vladimir Pcholkin/FPG International Corp.; **216**, *Shiva as Lord of the Dance*, The Asia Society, New York, Mr. and Mrs. John D. Rockefeller 3rd Collection/Photo by Lynton Gardiner; *Ravenna Apse Mosaic (Detail)*, Scala, Art Resource, New York; *The Pantheon*, ©Louis Grandadam/Tony Stone Images; *Hagia Sophia*, Constantinople (Istanbul, Turkey), ©The Stock Market/Harvey Lloyd; *The Great Stupa*, ©Hari Mahidhar/Dinodia Picture Agency; **217**, Page from *The Book of Lindisfarne*, Bridgeman/Art Resource, New York; *Pagoda of the Temple of the Six Banyan Trees*, Guangzhou, China, K. Scholz/H. Armstrong Roberts; *Great Mosque at Samarra*, Scala/Art Resource, New York; *Stupa at Borobudur*, Borromeo/Art Resource, New York; **218**, Rembrandt van Rijn, *Self-Portrait*, Andrew Mellon Collection, ©1996 Board of Trustees, National Gallery of Art, Washington, DC; Leonardo da Vinci, *Mona Lisa*, Louvre, Paris, France. Erich Lessing, Art Resource, NY; *Bayon Temple at Angkor Thom*, ©Josef Beck/FPG International Corp.; *Shrine Head*, The Minneapolis Institute of Arts, MN; Torii Kiyotada, *Actor of the Ichikawa Clan*, ©1979/94 The Metropolitan Museum of Art, New York, NY. Harris Brisbane Dick Fund, 1949. (JP3075); **219**, *Chartres Cathedral*, Scala/Art Resource, NY; Thomas Jefferson, *Monticello*, ©The Stock Market/ChromoSohm/Sohm, 1994; *Bayeux Tapestry (Detail)*, Musée de la Reine Mathilde, Bayeux, France. Erich Lessing/Art Resource, NY; *Taj Mahal*, ©The Telegraph Colour Library/FPG International Corp.; *Anasazi Culture Petroglyphs*, ©George H. H. Huey; **220**, Piet Mondrian, *Broadway Boogie-Woogie*, The Museum of Modern Art, New York, NY. Given anonymously. Photograph ©1988 The Museum of Modern Art, NY; Claude Monet, *Impression, Sunrise*, Musée Marmottan, Paris, France. Giraudon/Art Resource, NY; Edgar Degas, *Little Dancer of Fourteen*, Tate Gallery, London, England. Art Resource, NY; Katsushika Hokusai, *The Great Wave off Kanagawa*, The Metropolitan Museum of Art, New York, NY. H.O. Havemeyer Collection, Bequest of Mrs. H. O. Havemeyer, 1929; **221**, Pablo Picasso, *Gertrude Stein*, ©1996 The Metropolitan Museum of Art, New York, NY. Bequest of Gertrude Stein, 1946. (47.106); Chuck Close, *Self-Portrait*, Photograph courtesy Pace Wildenstein Gallery, New York, NY. Photo by Bill Jacobson; Jackson Pollock, *Convergence*, Albright-Knox Art Gallery, Buffalo, New York. Gift of Seymour H. Knox, 1956; Alexander Calder, *Untitled Mobile*, Gift of the Collectors Committee ©1996 Board of Trustees, National Gallery of Art, Washington, DC; Maria Martínez, *Black on Black Pots*, Courtesy of Maria Martínez, ©Jerry Jacka Photography; **228**, Aaron Haupt/Aaron Haupt Photography; **230**, Aaron Haupt/Aaron Haupt Photography; **232**, Simon Wilkinson/The Image Bar.

SRA/McGraw-Hill

*A Division of The **McGraw·Hill** Companies*

Copyright © 2001 by SRA/McGraw-Hill.

All rights reserved. Except as permitted under the United States Copyright Act, no part of this publication may be reproduced or distributed in any form or by any means, or stored in a database or retrieval system, without the prior written permission of the publisher, unless otherwise indicated.

Send all inquiries to:
SRA/McGraw-Hill
8787 Orion Place
Columbus, OH 43240-4027

Printed in the United States of America.

ISBN 0-02-684516-4

1 2 3 4 5 6 7 8 9 VHP 04 03 02 01 00

Authors

Senior Author
Dr. Rosalind Ragans, Ph. D.
Associate Professor Emerita
Georgia Southern University

Willis Bing Davis
Artist, Art Consultant
Former Art Department Chair
Central State University, Ohio

Tina Farrell
Director of Visual and
Performing Arts,
Clear Creek Independent School
District, Texas

Jane Rhoades Hudak, Ph.D.
Professor of Art
Georgia Southern University

Gloria McCoy
President,
Texas Art Education Association
K–12 Art Director, Spring Branch
Independent School District, Texas

Bunyan Morris
Art Teacher
Bulloch County School System,
Statesboro, Georgia

Nan Yoshida
Art Education Consultant,
Los Angeles, California

Contributors

ARTSOURCE Music,
Dance, Theater Lessons
Education Division
Performing Arts Center of
Los Angeles
Executive Director, Music Center
Education Division—Joan Boyett
Concept Originator and Project
Director—Melinda Williams
Project Coordinator—
Susan Cambigue-Tracey
Arts Discipline Writers:
Dance—Susan Cambigue-Tracey
Music—Rosemarie Cook-Glover
Theater—Barbara Leonard
Staff Assistance—Victoria Bernal
Logo Design—Maureen Erbe

More About Aesthetics

Richard W. Burrows,
Executive Director,
Institute for Arts Education,
San Diego, California

Safe Use of Art Materials

Mary Ann Boykin, Visiting Lecturer,
Art Education; Director, The Art
School for Children and Young Adults,
University of Houston-Clear Lake,
Houston, Texas

Museum Education

Marilyn JS Goodman,
Director of Education,
Solomon R. Guggenheim Museum,
New York, New York

The National Museum of Women in the Arts Collection

National Museum of
Women in the Arts,
Washington, DC

Contributing Writers

Dennis W. Black
High School Art Teacher
Clear Creek Independent
School District
Houston, TX

Jackie Ellett
Elementary Art Teacher
Fort Daniel Elementary School
Dacula, GA

Reviewers

Leslie Anderson
Teacher
Canopy Oaks Elementary School
Tallahassee, FL

Mary Ann Boykin
Visiting Lecturer, Art Education;
Director, The Art School for Children
and Young Adults
University of Houston-Clear Lake
Houston, TX

Theresa Davis
Art Specialist
Fleming Island Elementary
Clay County School District
Orange Park, FL

Judy Gong
Multi-age Classroom Teacher
Pacific Elementary School
Lincoln Unified School District
Stockton, CA

Lori Groendyke Knutti
Art Educator
Harrison Street Elementary School
Big Walnut Elementary School
Sunbury, OH

Laura McFadden
Art Supervisor
Briggs Elementary School
Florence District 1
Florence, SC

Steven R. Sinclair
Art Teacher
Big Country Elementary School
Southwest Independent School
District
San Antonio, TX

Connie Courtney Stephenson
Fine Arts Supervisor
Collier County School District
Naples, FL

Patti Wheeler
Teacher
N.B. Cook Elementary
School of the Arts
Escambia School District
Pensacola, FL

Student Activity Testers

Cassie Siler
Sara Gaul
Sabrina Trotter
Charlotte Jobrack
Brenna Wirtz
Jenna Taylor
Jamie Kintz
Abbie Kulju

TABLE OF CONTENTS

Unit 1

Line, Shape, and Value

Unit 2

Color, Rhythm, and Movement

Table of Contents
(continued)

Unit 3 — Space, Form, and Texture

Unit 4 — Proportion and Distortion

Table of Contents
(continued)

Unit 5 — Balance and Perspective

Unit 6 — Emphasis, Variety, Harmony, and Unity

Table of Contents
(continued)

More About . . .

What Is Art?

Art is . . .

Art is made by people

- to communicate ideas.
- to express feelings.
- to give us well-designed objects.

Painting

Painting is color applied to a flat surface.

Edward Hopper. (American). *House by the Railroad.* 1925. Oil on canvas. 24 x 29 inches. The Museum of Modern Art, New York, New York.

Drawing

Drawing is the process of making art with lines.

Wendy Fay Dixon. (American). *Deidre.* 1982. Silverpoint drawing on video paper. $17\frac{3}{4}$ x 17 inches. National Museum of Women in the Arts. Washington, DC.

Sculpture

Sculpture is art that fills space.

Duane Hanson. (American). *Football Player.* 1981. Oil on polyvinyl. $43\frac{1}{4}$ x 30 x $31\frac{1}{2}$ inches. Museum purchase through funds from the Friends of Art and public subscriptions, 82.0024. © Lowe Art Museum, University of Miami, all rights reserved.

Architecture

Architecture is the art of designing and constructing buildings.

Frank Lloyd Wright. (American). *Fallingwater.* 1936–1939. Bear Run, Pennsylvania. Glen Allison/Tony Stone Images © 1998 © 1996 Artists Rights Society (ARS), NY/Frank Lloyd Wright Foundation.

Printmaking

Printmaking is a process in which an original image is transferred from one prepared surface to another.

Käthe Kollwitz. (German). *The Downtrodden*. 1900. Etching. $9\frac{3}{4}$ x $12\frac{1}{8}$ inches. The National Museum of Women in the Arts, Washington, DC. Gift of Wallace and Wilhelmina Holladay/ © 1998 Artists Rights Society (ARS), New York/Bild-Kunst, Bonn.

Photography

Photography is the act of capturing an image on film.

Jerome Liebling. (American). *Young Boy, Minneapolis*. 1964. Photograph. 10 x 8 inches. The Minnesota Historical Society, St. Paul, Minnesota. ©Jerome Liebling Photography.

Ceramics

Ceramics is the art of making objects with clay.

Artist unknown. (Spain). *Deep Dish/Spain/from Valencia*. 1430. Tin-glazed earthenware painted in cobalt blue and lustre. 6.7 x 48.2 cm. Hispanic Society of America, New York, New York. Courtesy of Hispanic Society of America.

Jewelry

Jewelry is art to be worn.

Iris Sandkühler. (American). *Pyrite Sun Pendant (Detail)*. 1992. Copper, brass, pyrite, sterling, glass, base metal. 7 x 4 inches. Photograph: Sandkühler. Private Collection.

. . . and much more.

Art is a language.

The words of the language are the elements of art.

Line

Shape

Color

VALUE

SPACE

FORM

TEXTURE

Artists organize these words, or elements, using the principles of art.

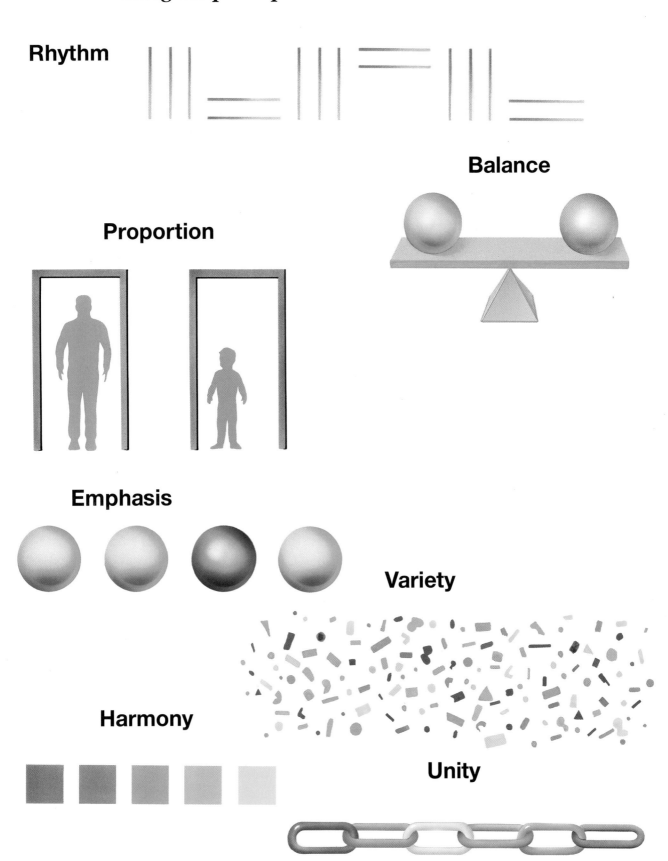

Rhythm

Balance

Proportion

Emphasis

Variety

Harmony

Unity

Every work of art has three parts.

They are

SUBJECT

The objects you can recognize are the subject matter of a work of art. When a work has no recognizable objects, the elements of art such as lines, shapes, colors, and so on become the subject of the work.

COMPOSITION

The composition of the work is the way the artist has used the principles to organize the elements of art.

CONTENT

The content is the message the artwork communicates. Content is the meaning of the work. If the work is functional, such as a chair or clothing, then the content is the function of the object.

Vincent van Gogh. (Dutch). *A Pair of Boots*. 1887. Oil on canvas. 13 x $16\frac{1}{8}$ inches. Baltimore Museum of Art, Baltimore, Maryland. The Cone Collection.

Artist unknown. Navajo, (United States). *Navajo blanket, Eye Dazzler*. Dallas Museum of Art, Dallas, Texas, Textile Purchase Fund.

Elizabeth Plater-Zyberk. (American). *Seaside, Florida. A Walkway.* Andres Duany & Elizabeth Plater-Zyberk.

Edgar Degas. (French). *At the Milliner's.* 1882. Pastel on paper. 30 x 34 inches. Metropolitan Museum of Art, New York City, New York.

In which work of art do you think the subject matter is very important?

In which artwork do you think composition is most important?

Which work seems to have the strongest message? Explain.

Which artwork's meaning relates to its function?

An Introduction to
Line, Shape, and Value

Line, shape, and value are used by artists to create many types of art.

Jaune Quick-to-See Smith. (American). *Rainbow.* 1989. Oil and mixed-media on canvas. 66 × 84 inches. Private Collection/Courtesy Steinbaum Krauss Gallery, New York, New York.

Artists use **lines** in a work of art to create movement and shapes.

- What area of the picture do your eyes see first? Where do they end up last?
- What types of lines do you see? Do you see any of these lines more than once?

Shapes are used by artists to create objects or people.

- What shapes do you see in this painting?

Artist Profile

Jaune Quick-to-See Smith
1940–

Jaune Quick-to-See Smith grew up on a Montana reservation. Her Shoshone grandmother gave her the name "Quick-to-See" because she was quick to understand things. As a child, she often went on long trips with her father, who was a horse trainer and trader. She saw the beauty of the rugged northwestern landscape and was inspired to draw. Her paintings reflect her concern about the destruction of the environment and Native American cultures.

Jaune Quick-to-See Smith and other artists use line and value to help create movement and shapes. In this unit you will learn and practice how artists use line, shape, and value to create art. Here are the techniques.

- Types of Lines
- Shapes
- Value

Lines

Artists use different kinds of lines to create shapes and express attitudes and ideas.

The *Huipil Weaving* is part of a garment made and worn by the Cakchiquel Maya of Guatemala. Charles Sheeler painted *Incantation* to show the huge machines commonly found in an industrial plant. Notice that both artists use a variety of lines in their work. See how many different kinds of lines you can find in each work. Look for lines that are repeated.

Maya/Huipil (detail) plate 263. c. 1950. Backstrap woven plain weave with supplementary—weft pattern, silk on cotton. 50 × 14½ inches. From the Girard Foundation Collection, in the Museum of International Folk Art, a unit of the Museum of New Mexico, Santa Fe, Photographer: Michel Monteaux.

Charles Sheeler.
(American).
Incantation. 1946.
Oil on canvas.
24 × 20 inches. The
Brooklyn Museum,
Brooklyn, New York.
John B. and
Ella C. Woodward
Memorial Funds.

Study both the weaving and the painting to find a variety of lines.

- ✓ Look for lines that move up and down and side to side.

- ✓ Do you see a line that zigzags?

- ✓ Which lines slant?

- ✓ How do the lines help create a mood?

- ✓ Compare both works of art. Do you see lines that are similar?

SEEING LIKE AN ARTIST

Look around for various lines in the furniture and in your classmates' clothing. Find lines like the ones you saw in the weaving and painting.

Lesson 1

Using Lines

A **line** is a mark drawn by a tool such as a pencil, pen, or paintbrush as it moves across a surface. There are five different kinds of lines. Lines have different lengths, widths, and textures. Some curve and move in different directions.

 Vertical lines move up and down, creating a feeling of strength and stability.

 Horizontal lines move side to side, creating a calm feeling.

 Diagonal lines move at a slant and are full of energy.

 **Zigzag** lines are made by joining diagonal direction lines.

 **Curved** lines bend and change gradually or turn inward to form spirals.

Lines can be **long** or **short**, **thick** or **thin**, or **rough** or **smooth**.

Practice

Draw each line and its variations. Use markers.

1. Fold a sheet of paper into six equal boxes. Print the name of each of the five types of lines at the top of each box, leaving one box empty.

2. Using a black marker, create the type of line indicated.

3. In the empty box, write your favorite type of line.

Decide Did you use all five types of lines correctly? Did you vary the thickness, length, and texture? What directional lines did you create?

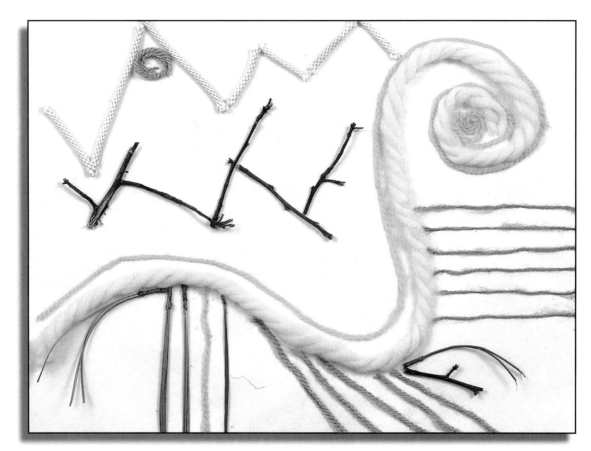

Aaron Robbins. Age 11. *Line Party*. Mixed-media on posterboard.

What lines and line variations did the student artist use in this mixed media collage?

Create

In what other way can you make lines besides drawing them? Create a mixed-media collage using lines.

1. Think about the five different types of lines. Collect linear mixed-media materials such as yarn, string, or grass.

2. Use different materials to create lines and line variations. Keep in mind the mood that certain lines suggest.

3. Arrange and glue the collage materials onto a piece of cardboard background.

Describe What lines and materials did you use in your collage?

Analyze Why did you choose certain materials for certain lines? How did you combine your lines?

Interpret What would you title the collage?

Decide Were you successful in creating a variety of lines? If you could do this collage over again, how would you change it?

Geometric and Free-Form Shapes

Artists use a variety of geometric and free-form shapes to convey an idea and to represent natural objects and artificial objects.

Joan Miró. (Spanish). *The Beautiful Bird Revealing the Unknown to a Pair of Lovers.* 1941. Gouache and oil wash on paper. 18 × 15 inches. The Museum of Modern Art, New York, New York. Acquired through the Lillie P. Bliss Bequest. Photograph © 1998. Artist Rights Society (ARS), New York/ADAGP, Paris.

Miró did not paint realistic-looking objects. He created a lively design of a variety of lines and shapes. Paul Wonner placed natural objects next to artificial ones. Both Miró and Wonner use a variety of shapes and lines in their paintings to express themselves.

Paul Wonner. (American).
Dutch Still Life with Art Books and Field Guide to Western Birds.
1982. Acrylic on canvas.
72 × 50 inches. Hunter Museum of American Art, Chattanooga, Tennessee. Museum purchase with funds from the Benwood Foundation and the 1983 Collector's Group.

Study both paintings to find a variety of shapes.

- ✓ Where do you see circles, squares, rectangles, or triangles in either work?

- ✓ Do you see a shape with five, six, or eight sides?

- ✓ Find irregular shapes made with curved lines.

- ✓ Point to shapes made with color and created with outlines.

SEEING LIKE AN ARTIST

Turn a book around in your hands. How many shapes can you see as you look at it from different angles?

Using Geometric and Free-Form Shapes

Shapes are two-dimensional figures and can be measured in two ways—by height and width. A shape may have an outline or boundary around it, or it can be a solid color like a shadow. There are two kinds of shapes.

Geometric shapes are shapes that can be described using mathematical formulas. They are shapes with names. The three basic geometric shapes are the square, the circle, and the triangle. When you combine them you create **complex geometric shapes** such as those below.

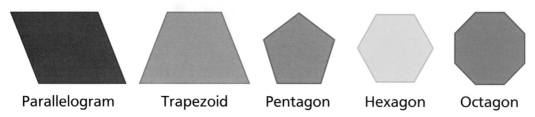

Parallelogram   Trapezoid   Pentagon   Hexagon   Octagon

Geometric shapes are usually seen in objects made by people such as buildings and machines.

Free-form shapes are uneven and irregular. They can be made with curved lines, straight lines, or a combination of the two. They are most often found in nature.

Practice

Create cutout geometric shapes. Use cut paper.

1. Cut out basic shapes such as circles, squares, and triangles.

2. Experiment with the cutout shapes to create complex geometric shapes.

Decide What are the complex geometric shapes you created? How did you make them?

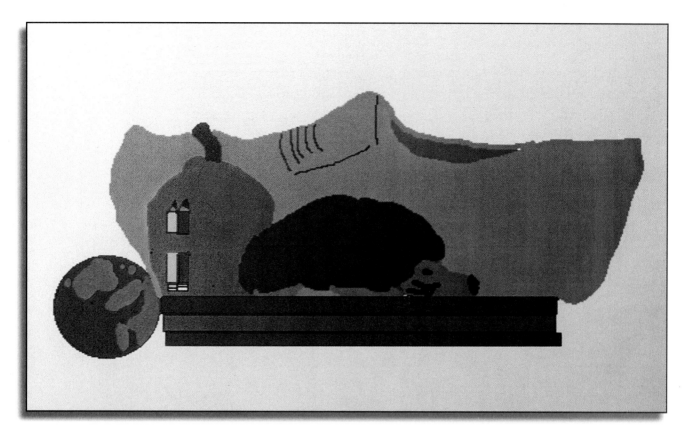

Austin Reedy. Age 12. *Teacher's Desk.* Computer paint program.

What geometric and free-form shapes do you see in this student artist's still life?

Create

Look around you for objects that have both geometric and free-form shapes. Draw a still life on the computer using geometric and free-form shapes.

1. Think about objects you might enjoy drawing. Select five or more of different sizes and shapes and arrange them.

2. Practice using the pencil ✎, paintbrush 🖌, and fill 🪣 tools in your computer program.

3. Using the pencil ✎ tool, draw your still life on the computer. Add color and textures using the paintbrush 🖌 and fill 🪣 tools.

4. Save your finished drawing. Print your final work.

Describe What objects did you use? What lines, shapes, and colors did you use?

Analyze How did you use lines and color to create shapes?

Interpret What is the main idea or mood of your drawing?

Decide Were you able to see a variety of shapes in the still life you set up?

Value in Shading

Artists use shading to create highlights and shadows
so that an object looks more realistic.

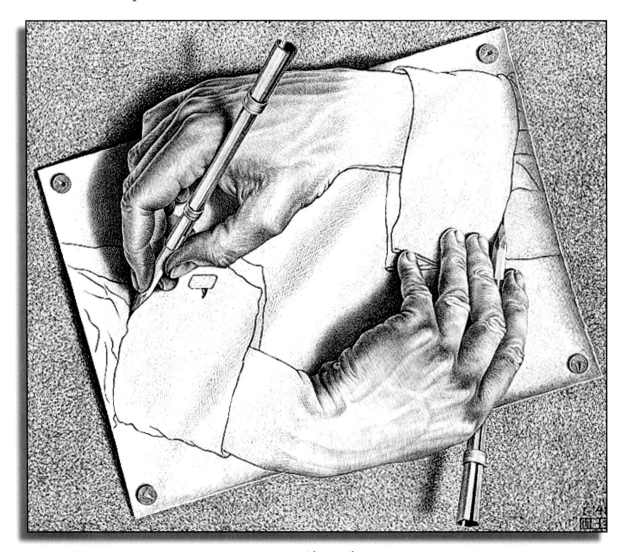

M.C. Escher. (Dutch). *Drawing Hands.* 1948. $11\frac{1}{8} \times 13\frac{1}{8}$ inches. Escher book Lithograph.
Cornelius van S. Roosevelt Collection, © 1996 Board of Trustees, National Gallery of Art,
Washington, DC.

M.C. Escher creates the illusion of two hands drawing
each other. His hands begin as a line drawing, but he
gradually darkens and lightens to create the illusion of hands
coming to life. Dixon uses a sharpened silver wire to draw the
image of a face peering through fish. She draws on special
paper, and as the silver ages and tarnishes, the drawing
darkens. Both artists used areas of light and dark to create
the illusion of reality in these fantasy pictures.

Wendy Fay Dixon. (American). *Deidre*. 1982. Silverpoint on paper.
$17\frac{3}{4} \times 17$ inches. The National Museum of Women in the Arts,
Washington, DC. Gift of Deidre Busenberg and the artist.

Examine how both artists used value.

✓ Where are the darkest and lightest areas in each picture?

✓ Where are you in relation to the picture?

✓ How did the artists make certain objects look realistic?

SEEING LIKE AN ARTIST
Slowly turn your hand and observe how the light and dark areas change as your hand turns.

Using Value

Value is the lightness and darkness of a color or object. The values of an object change according to the way the light strikes it. As it is turned, its values change according to the point of view or angle.

 **Shading** is a technique for darkening values by adding black or darkening an area by repeating several lines close together.

 **Gradation** is a gradual change from one value to another.

Point of view is the position from which the viewer looks at an object.

When you look at an object from different points of view, its shape and values appear to change.

Practice

Draw a value scale. Use a soft lead pencil and white paper.

1. Draw seven boxes. Leave the first box white, and color the last box black.

2. Practice shading in the other boxes to create different values. Make light pencil marks closest to the white box and darker values closest to the black box.

Decide Were you able to create a value scale going gradually from white to black?

Abbie Kulju. Age 10. *The Clay Pot.* Oil pastel and charcoal.

How does the form of the pitcher change in each view of this student artwork?

Create

Why does the form of an object change when the point of view changes? Draw one object from three different points of view.

1. Think about how to use shading to show form in drawing. Draw a three-dimensional object from three points of view. Move it around under a direct light source.

2. Shade to indicate form. Use lead pencil for detail, and an eraser to lighten.

Describe How does the shape of the shadows change in each point of view?

Analyze How did you create shadows and highlights?

Interpret How does strong light and shadow affect the look of the work?

Decide Do you think strong light and shadow is an interesting way to show form?

Value in Lines

Artists use lines to create values in a work of art.

Elizabeth Catlett. (American). *Sharecropper.* 1970. Color linocut.
26 × 22 inches. National Museum of American Art, Smithsonian Institution,
Washington, DC. ©1998 Elizabeth Catlett/Licensed by VAGA, New York, NY.

Elizabeth Catlett's print is a linoleum cut. She uses a sharp tool to cut lines in a linoleum plate. The cut lines do not hold ink and appear white in the printed image. Käthe Kollwitz's etching was created by using acid to etch lines into a metal plate. The lines held ink and appear black in the printed image. Both artists use a variety of lines and patterns to create different values in their compositions.

Käthe Kollwitz. (German). *The Downtrodden*. Etching.
$9\frac{3}{4} \times 12\frac{1}{8}$ inches. The National Museum of Women in the Arts,
Washington DC. Gift of Wallace and Wilhelmina Holladay. 1998
Artists Rights Society (ARS), New York/VG Bild-Kunst, Bonn.

Study both prints to find out how lines are used to create values.

- ✓ What types of lines do you see?

- ✓ Where are lines close together or far apart?

- ✓ Which areas have dark values and which have light values?

- ✓ How did the two artists create these feelings or emotions?

SEEING LIKE AN ARTIST

Find an example of repeated lines used to make an object darker. How does an artist create a light area on an object?

Line and Value

The darkness or lightness of an object refers to its **value**. Line patterns create different values. When lines are placed side by side, or parallel, value is created. The closer together parallel lines are, the darker the value. The farther apart the lines are placed, the lighter the value.

Hatching is used to create shading values by using a series of fine parallel lines.

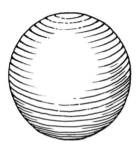 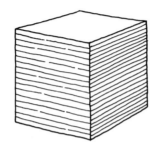 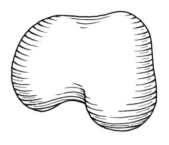

Cross-hatching is used to create shading values by using two or more intersecting sets of parallel lines.

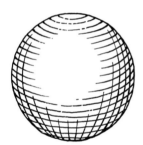 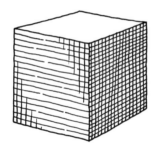 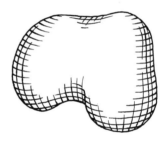

Hatching and cross-hatching are used for shading. The closer together your lines are, the darker your artwork will appear.

Practice

Draw a value scale using parallel lines. Use a pencil.

1. Draw a rectangle and divide it into five sections.

2. Draw parallel lines far apart in one section to show the lightest value. Draw lines as close as you can without having them touch to show the darkest value.

Decide Were you successful in drawing parallel lines to create a value scale going from light to dark?

Dominique Belle. Age 11. *Zephanie.* Pencil.

What techinique does the student artist use to create values in the drawing?

Create

How can you use lines in drawing to show different values? Use shading techniques to create values in a drawing.

1. Think about ways to draw emotions on a face. Make sketches of a person's face close-up. Show a different emotion in each sketch.

2. Choose one sketch. Make it simple and use a variety of shading techniques such as crosshatching and hatching to create value in your drawing.

Describe Describe the shading techniques you used.

Analyze How did you use value to emphasize emotion in your drawing?

Interpret What emotion did you create in your drawing? Give your work a title.

Decide Were you successful in using shading techniques to create different values?

Value

Artists sometimes use lighting to create highlights
and shadows in their artwork.

Diego Rivera. (Mexican). *Dance in Tehuantepec.* 1935. (M.74.22.4) Charcoal and watercolor.
$18\frac{15}{16} \times 23\frac{7}{8}$ inches. (48.10 x 60.64 cm) Los Angeles County Museum of Art, Los Angeles,
California. Gift of Mr. and Mrs. Milton W. Lipper from the Milton W. Lipper Estate.
Reproduction authorized by the National Institute of Fine Arts and Literature.

Four dancers in Diego Rivera's drawing are dancing
the Zandunga, a popular folk dance in the Tehuantepec
region of Mexico. The painting by Renoir shows two girls
studying music at the piano. Notice how both artists use light
and shadow in their work.

Auguste Renoir. (French).
Two Young Girls at the Piano.
1892. Oil on canvas.
44 × 34 inches. Metropolitan
Museum of Art, Robert
Lehman Collection, 1975.
New York, New York.

Study both paintings for their use of light and shadow.

☑ Find the lightest and darkest areas in both works of art.

☑ How do the light and shadows affect the look of the clothing?

☑ How does the use of light and shadow create a mood in each work?

SEEING LIKE AN ARTIST
Think about how you would draw the natural lighting and shadows you see in your classroom.

Using Value

The darkness or lightness of an object is described by its **value**. Value depends on how much light a surface reflects. Artists often draw a scene by creating a perception drawing using highlights and shadows.

Perception is the act of looking at something carefully and thinking deeply about what is seen.

Shadows are the shaded areas in a drawing or painting. They show the surfaces of the subject that reflect the least amount of light. They create the illusion of form or depth and dimension.

Highlights are small areas of white or light values used to show the very brightest spots. They are the opposites of shadows, and they help create illusion of form.

Practice

Illustrate highlight and shadow. Use pencil.

1. Drape a piece of solid-colored fabric over a chair in front of the classroom.

2. Shine a strong light or spotlight on the fabric. Lightly sketch part of the fabric with a pencil. Pay careful attention to highlights and shadows.

Decide How did you create the highlights and shadows?

Heather McAllister. Age 11. *The Princess.* Pencil.

Where is the strong light coming from in this drawing? Where are the highlights? Where are the darkest shadows?

Create

How can you use value to introduce highlights and dark shadows in a figure drawing? Use value techniques in a drawing.

1. Think about the mood that is created with the use of light. Put a spotlight or strong light on two costumed volunteers from your class.

2. Use shading and perception to draw them. Look at the highlights and dark shadows on the faces and costumes. Make several sketches on gray paper using charcoal and white chalk.

Describe Describe what you included in your drawing.

Analyze What areas have highlights and shadows?

Interpret How did the highlights and shadows affect the mood?

Decide Were you successful in creating highlights and dark shadows? What might you do to improve your drawing?

Value Contrast

Photographers use light to create contrast and to emphasize the subject.

Jerome Liebling. (American). *Young Boy, Minneapolis.* 1964.
Photograph. 10 x 8 inches. The Minnesota Historical Society,
St. Paul, Minnesota. © Jerome Liebling Photography.

Both photographers use strong value contrast to tell
their stories about the American scene. Liebling
uses the contrast between light and dark values to
emphasize the reflective mood of the boy in the photo.
Steiner contrasts the chair against its shadow on the
wooden porch to create his visual story about a specific
time and place.

Ralph Steiner. (American). *American Rural Baroque.* 1930. Gelatin-silver print. $7\frac{9}{16} \times 9\frac{1}{2}$ inches. Museum of Modern Art, New York, New York.

Study the two photographs carefully to see value contrast.

✓ Where do you see the darkest and lightest values in both photographs?

✓ Do you see any areas where a highlight is next to a dark shadow?

✓ How do the values tell you about the time of day each photograph was taken?

✓ How did each artist use value to create or emphasize a mood?

SEEING LIKE AN ARTIST

Look around your classroom. Are there areas of strong light next to dark, shadowed areas like the ones in the photographs?

Creating Value Contrast

The darkness or lightness of an object is its **value**. Value depends on how much light a surface reflects. Contrast is often created when working with values. **Contrast** is the degree of difference between color values, tones, shapes, and other elements in works of art. Shading techniques such as stippling, cross-hatching, and hatching lines can help create value contrast in a drawing.

     Hatching is made by using a series of repeated parallel lines.

     Cross-hatching is created when two or more sets of parallel lines cross each other.

     Stippling is done by shading with dots. The closer the dots, the darker the area.

Practice

Practice creating contrast in a drawing. Use a black marker.

1. Divide a sheet of paper into three sections. Label each section a shading technique: hatching, cross-hatching, and stippling.

2. Draw a different shape in each box and practice the different shading techniques.

Decide How did you create contrast in your drawing?

Shavonta Johnson. Age 11. *The Oriental Tale*. Photograph.

How does the student artist create value contrast in the photograph?

Create

Where do you see value contrast in your environment? Create a photograph that has both bright highlights and dark shadows, and have it tell a story or express a mood.

1. Look around your indoor and outdoor environment. Find an interesting area, with objects or people, that tells a story or expresses a mood.

2. Use a camera. Look through the viewfinder to arrange your composition. Be sure that your photograph will have bright highlights and dark shadows. Take your photograph.

3. Have your photograph developed. Share it with the class.

Describe Describe the objects and spaces you included in your photograph.

Analyze Does your photograph have highlights and shadows? Where are they? Do your values change gradually or quickly?

Interpret Give your photograph an expressive title.

Decide Were you successful in creating a photograph that has strong value contrast and also tells a story or expresses a mood?

Lesson 6

Lines, Shapes, and Forms in a Tableau

Classic Journeys or Tableau of Contents: *David Novak.*

a tableau is like a still-life photograph, except that the people shown are alive and breathing. Like a photograph, a tableau captures a moment or scene and freezes it. The scene may tell a story or express an emotion or a mood, such as courage or joy. In this living still life, observers can see a variety of lines, shapes, and forms.

What To Do

Create a tableau, or "living photograph," to communicate a theme.

Materials
- ✔ pencils
- ✔ paper

1. Make a list of some themes and values such as family, freedom, love, joy, justice, beauty, and nature.

2. Work in a group. Choose an idea from the list. Try different ways to show that theme using poses, closeness or distance to each other, and facial expressions.

3. Select a pose that communicates the idea. Assume the positions in your tableau and then freeze.

4. Choose a title for your tableau. To perform, use a count of three beats to get into position. Freeze for five beats. Finally, release the "freeze" and stand straight with your hands at your sides.

Describe Describe the tableau you created.

Analyze Explain how you used lines, shapes, and forms to express your theme.

Interpret What mood or feelings did your tableau express?

Decide How well do you think you succeeded in communicating your theme?

Extra Credit

Work with a partner or in a small group. Choose a famous painting or other well-known artwork and re-create it in a tableau. Perform it for the class.

Line, Shape, and Value

Reviewing Main Ideas

The lessons and activities in Unit 1 are based on how artists use line, shape, and value to create works of art.

- **Line —** When a dot moves and creates a path through space. Although there are five different kinds of lines, all lines move in only three directions.

    1. **Vertical** lines move up and down, creating a feeling of strength and stability.

    2. **Horizontal** lines move side to side, creating a calm feeling.

3. **Diagonal** lines move at a slant and are full of energy.

- **Shapes** are flat, or two-dimensional. They can be measured by length and by height. All shapes can be categorized into one of two groups.

    1. **Free-form** shapes have uneven or irregular edges. They are most often found in nature.

Isabel Bishop. (American). *Men and Girls Walking.* 1969. Aquatint on paper. $8\frac{3}{8} \times 11\frac{1}{2}$ inches. National Museum of Women in the Arts, Washington, DC. Gift of Mr. and Mrs. Edward P. Levy.

2. **Geometric** shapes can be described using mathematical formulas. The three basic geometric shapes are the square, circle, and triangle.

- **Value** is the lightness and darkness of a color or object. There are three ways to create value.
  1. **Shading** is a technique for darkening values by adding black or repeating several lines close together.
  2. **Gradation** is a gradual change of one value to another—from light to dark or dark to light.
  3. **Highlights and shadows** are opposites of each other. Highlights are small areas of white or light values to show bright spots. Shadows are shaded areas that reflect the smallest amount of light.

Summing Up

Isabel Bishop used line, shape, and value to capture the scenes she observed from her studio window in New York City.

- What lines do you see in the artwork?
- What basic shapes did Bishop use to create the figures you see?
- How does the artist create value in the artwork?

Line, shape, and value are all important art elements that artists use to convey a feeling or make a statement. Artists use these art elements to create two-dimensional works of art.

Careers in Art
Medical Illustrator

Marsha Jessup has a profession that combines two of her favorite things—biology and art. Medical illustrators are artists who work in the field of medicine. When Jessup was 14, her mother, who is also an artist, suggested she consider medical illustration as a career. Jessup's training included four years of premedical studies, many courses in art, and a graduate degree in medical illustration. Today she works in Piscataway, New Jersey, combining administrative responsibilities with training people in biomedical computer imaging.

Marsha Jessup

Unit 2

An Introduction to
Color, Rhythm, and Movement

Many artists use color and visual rhythm to create drawings, paintings, prints, and sculptures.

Claude Monet. (French). *Rouen Cathedral, West Facade, Sunlight.* 1894. Oil on canvas. $50\frac{1}{4} \times 36$ inches. Chester Dale Collection, © 1996 Board of Trustees, National Gallery of Art, Washington, DC.

Artists use **color** to express a mood or feeling in their artwork.

• What colors do you see in this painting?

• Monet wanted to express the feeling and quality of light in his paintings. He did this by using dabs of soft colors rather than filling large areas with solid bright colors. How would changing the colors of the painting make it different?

Rhythm is used by artists to create a feeling of movement and add visual excitement to a piece of artwork.

• What shapes do you see repeated in the painting? What color are the shapes?

Artist Profile

Claude Monet
1840–1926

Claude Monet was born in Paris, France. He is recognized as one of the first artists to paint outdoors rather than in a painting studio. Monet painted this scene of Rouen Cathedral more than 30 times. He worked on each painting at a different time of day so that he could better understand the effect of light on color.

Claude Monet and other artists use color to express a mood or feeling. Many artists also use color to create contrast and visual excitement. In this unit you will learn and practice the techniques that artists use to create color and visual rhythm in their artwork. These are the techniques.

• Color Schemes   • Visual Rhythm   • Value   • Contrast

Monochromatic Colors

Artists use monochromatic colors to bring together or unite their artwork visually.

Ben Jones. (American). *King Family.* 1980. Mixed media. 30 × 40 inches. Collection of the Studio Museum, Harlem, New York.

The *King Family* is a drawing created by Ben Jones. His work shows the faces of familiar people like the Dr. Martin Luther King, Jr., family. Jasper Johns created his collage and wax-based painting *Map* about the map of the United States. His style emphasizes media rather than subject matter. Notice how both artists use color to unify their work.

Jasper Johns. (American). *Map*. 1962. Encaustic and collage on canvas. 60 × 93 inches. The Museum of Contemporary Art, Los Angeles, California. Collection of the Marcia Simon Weisman Trust, partial gift to the Museum of Contemporary Art, Los Angeles, California. ©Johns/VAGA, 1993.

Study the monochromatic color schemes in both pieces of artwork.

- What one color is used most often in each work of art?

- Where do you see colors that are lighter or darker than the main color?

- What type of lines and shapes do you see in each work of art?

- What feeling is expressed in each artwork? How did these artists create these feelings?

SEEING LIKE AN ARTIST

What objects in nature are made of only one color and variations of that color?

Using Monochromatic Colors

Monochromatic means "one color." A color scheme that is monochromatic uses only one color and the tints and shades of that color.

Hue is another name for color. Red, blue, and yellow are **primary hues**. By mixing primary hues, you get **secondary hues**. Red and blue make violet, red and yellow make orange, and blue and yellow make green. **Intermediate hues** are made by mixing a primary hue with an adjacent secondary hue. Red and orange make the intermediate color red-orange. A color wheel is the spectrum bent into a circle. The wheel below is a twelve-color wheel.

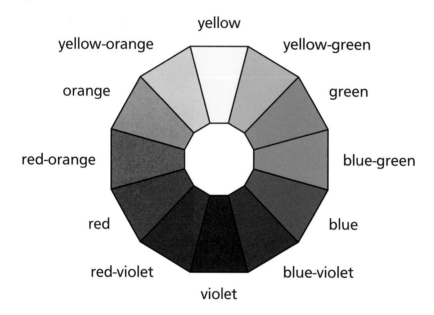

Tint is a light value of a hue made by adding white to a hue.
Shade is a dark value of a hue made by adding black to a hue.

Practice

**Practice mixing monochromatic colors.
Use tempera paint.**

1. Draw three squares. Label the first "hue," the second "tint," and the third "shade." Paint each square.

2. Create a tint in the second square and a shade in the third square.

3. Experiment to create various values of the primary hue.

Decide Did you create monochromatic colors of one primary hue?

Dustin Sandidge. Age 11. *Night City.* Tempera.

How does the monochromatic color scheme affect the mood of the artwork?

Create

What color dominates your favorite real or imaginary scene? Paint a real or imaginary scene using tints and shades of one hue.

1. Think about imaginary places and real places. Select one place and make several simple sketches of it.

2. Select your best sketch. Draw it lightly.

3. Mix one hue with white and black paint to create a variety of tints and shades. Paint your scene using a monochromatic color scheme.

Describe Describe your scene. Is it imaginary or realistic?

Analyze What hue did you choose? Describe the tints and the shades of that hue.

Interpret What kind of mood did you create?

Decide Were you successful in creating a monochromatic scene?

Analogous Colors

Artists use analogous color schemes in their
paintings to tie various shapes together.

Georgia O'Keeffe. (American).
Red and Pink Rocks and Teeth. 1938.
Oil on canvas. 53.5 × 33 cm. The Art
Institute of Chicago, Chicago, Illinois.
Gift of Georgia O'Keeffe, © 1998 The
Georgia O'Keeffe Foundation/Artists
Rights Society (ARS), New York.

Georgia O'Keeffe was interested in painting things
that were uniquely American. She used colors found in
the New Mexico desert. *Eye Dazzler* is a Navajo blanket. The
Navajo of New Mexico are noted for their intricate weavings.
Both the painting and the blanket use related colors to bring
various shapes and lines together.

Artist unknown. Navajo Tribe (United States).
Navajo Blanket Eye Dazzler. 1890. Wool, cotton;
tapestry weave; slit tapestry; dovetailed tapestry.
75 × 57 inches. Dallas Museum of Art, Dallas, Texas.
Textile Purchase Fund.

Study both works of art to find analogous colors.

✓ Find the red colors in the painting and the blanket.

✓ What orange areas or lines do you see in each work?

✓ Where are the dark red colors in each work?

✓ What shapes do you see in both works of art?

✓ Find areas in both pieces that are lighter and darker
than the main color.

SEEING LIKE AN ARTIST

Find objects or
clothing in which
similar colors are used.
What colors do you
see in the painting and
the blanket?

Using Analogous Colors

On the color wheel, **analogous colors** sit next to each other. They share a common color or hue. For example, violet, blue, blue-green, and green are analogous colors. They share the color blue and are next to each other on the color wheel.

A **color scheme** is a plan for organizing colors. Analogous colors are one type of color scheme. The color scheme on the left shares the color blue. The color scheme on the right shares the color red.

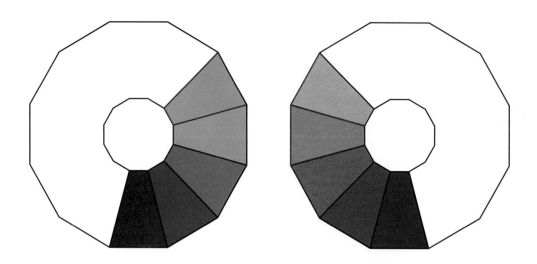

Practice

Create a color wheel using primary, secondary, and intermediate colors. Use paint.

1. Draw a large circle and divide it into 12 equal pie-shaped wedges. Paint a primary color in every fourth wedge.

2. Combine primary colors to make secondary colors. Paint the appropriate secondary color in the middle wedge of each empty section. Mix secondary colors with primary colors to create intermediate colors. Paint the appropriate intermediate color in the remaining wedges.

Decide Did you mix secondary and intermediate colors? How can you improve them?

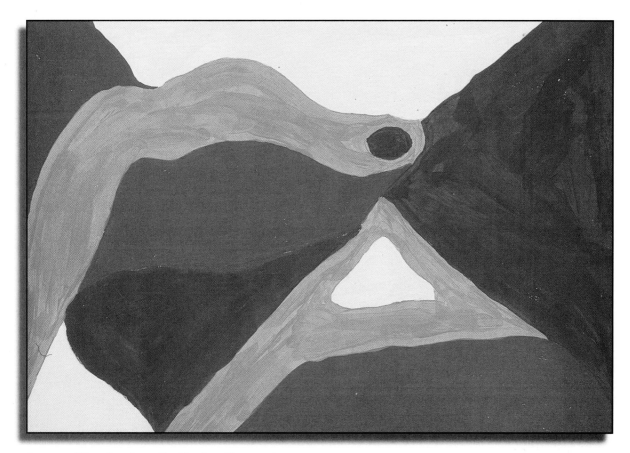

James Woods. Age 10. *Singing Shapes*. Tempera.

What set of analogous colors did the student artist use in this nonobjective painting?

Create

What are the different shapes you see in your environment? Create a nonobjective painting with an analogous color scheme.

1. Think about different shapes. Draw shapes that overlap and vary in size. Draw several sketches.

2. Reproduce one design to create a nonobjective painting. A **nonobjective painting** contains shapes, lines, and colors, not objects or people.

3. Use an analogous color scheme to paint your nonobjective design.

Describe What type of shapes did you use in your nonobjective painting?

Analyze Name the analogous colors you used in your painting.

Interpret What title best reflects the mood of your artwork?

Decide Did you successfully create a nonobjective painting using analogous colors?

Complementary Colors

Artists use complementary colors to create contrast and visual excitement in their artwork.

Artist unknown. (Peru). *Featherwork Neckpiece.* 1350–1476. $13\frac{1}{4} \times 11\frac{1}{2}$ inches. Cotton, feathers, beads; Late Intermediate Period; China Style. Dallas Museum of Art. The Eugene and Margaret McDermott Art Fund, Inc.

The *Featherwork Neckpiece* is an example of an adornment. An **adornment** decorates or adds beauty to an object or a person. Willis Bing Davis uses historical African patterns and forms as inspiration for his contemporary images. In Davis's work, he reflects on the images and feelings he experienced while attending a ritual dance in Nigeria. Notice that both artists used contrasting colors. What emotional qualities were they trying to express?

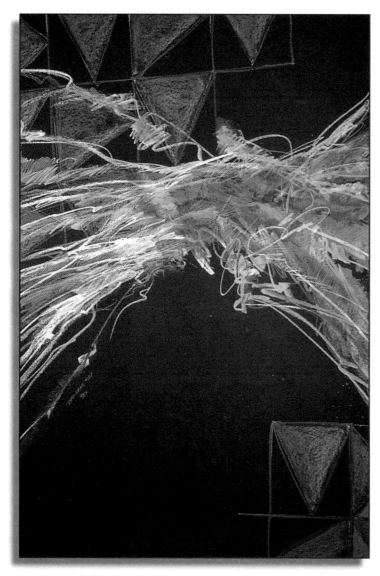

Willis Bing Davis. (American). *Ancestral Spirit Dance Series.*
60 × 40 inches. Courtesy of Willis Bing Davis.

Study both works of art to find their complementary color schemes.

✓ What colors do you see?

✓ Do you see different shades or tints of these colors?

✓ What colors do you see repeated?

✓ Talk about how the artists created contrast in the artwork.

SEEING LIKE AN ARTIST

Do you notice any classmates wearing colors that contrast or look bright next to each other? What colors are they wearing?

Using Complementary Colors

Colors opposite each other on the color wheel are called **complementary colors**. A complement of a color is the strongest contrast to the color. They are used to create contrast. Red and green, blue and orange, and violet and yellow are all complementary colors.

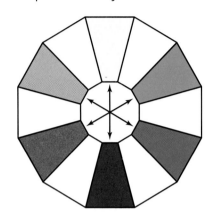

Complementary colors seem to vibrate when they are placed next to each other.

Color Intensities Mixing a color with its complement lowers the brightness of that color. When two complementary colors are mixed, the color becomes dull. Look at the intensity scale. As you add a small amount of green to red, it becomes dull. More green makes it duller. Equal amounts of red and green make an interesting low-intensity gray. The same thing happens when you add red to green.

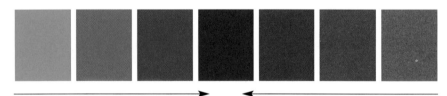

Practice

Experiment with pieces of colored paper to see how complementary colors affect each other. Use colored paper.

1. Cut out a hole in a piece of paper. Place the paper with the hole on top of the complementary color to see how they look.

2. Place the hole you cut out on top of the complementary color to see how it looks inside the color.

Decide How did the complementary colors affect each other?

Rusty Cartee. Age 11. *A Pickle Sandwich.* Construction paper and marker.

What set of complementary colors did the student artist use?

Create

What complementary colors would best communicate an idea or event you would like to advertise? Create a poster using complementary colors.

1. Think about an event or idea of interest to you. Create a poster to communicate it. Pick one set of complementary colors for your poster.

2. Using two complementary colors, cut out shapes, letters, and designs. Overlap shapes and have them touch the edges of the background.

3. Glue your shapes and letters onto the background.

Describe What complementary colors, objects, and shapes did you use?

Analyze How did your complementary colors create contrast and visual excitement?

Interpret What is the theme and mood of your poster?

Decide Did your poster successfully communicate your event or idea?

Warm and Cool Colors

Artists use warm and cool color schemes to create a mood or feeling in their artwork.

Robert Lostutter. (American). *Baird Trogon.* 1985. Watercolor over graphite. 61.5 × 88 cm. Art Institute of Chicago, Chicago, Illinois. Restricted Gift of the Illinois Arts Council, Logan Fund, 1985.

Lostutter uses the contrast of warm and cool colors to show his expertise with watercolors and his interest in birds. The textures of the feathers contrast with the smooth skin of the man. Mabe uses contrasts between lights and darks and blobs of color to express emotions in his work. Mabe was influenced by his oriental traditions. Both artists have used the contrast of warm and cool colors.

Manabu Mabe. (Brazilian). *Melancholy Metropolis*. 1961. Oil on canvas. $72\frac{7}{8} \times 78\frac{7}{8} \times 1\frac{1}{4}$ inches. Collection Walker Art Center, Minneapolis, Minnesota, Gift of the T. B. Walker Foundation 1963.

Study both paintings to find the warm and cool colors.

- ✓ What colors do you see that remind you of water, the forest, or a cool winter's day?

- ✓ What other colors do you see? Are there any colors that remind you of fire?

- ✓ How do these colors affect the mood of these paintings?

SEEING LIKE AN ARTIST

Notice the colors worn most often and least often in class. Do these colors remind you of something warm or something cool?

Using Warm and Cool Colors

Sometimes colors are divided into warm and cool colors. They make us think about warm or cool things when we see them.

Warm colors are red, orange, and yellow. They suggest warmth and seem to move toward the viewer. They remind us of the sun or fire. Artists use warm color schemes to express a warm mood.

Cool colors are blue, green, and violet. They suggest coolness and seem to move away from the viewer. Cool colors remind us of ice, water, and grass. Artists use cool color schemes to express a cool mood.

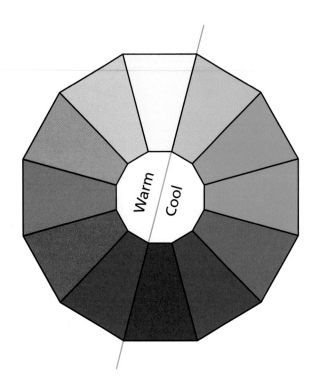

Practice

Experiment with warm and cool colors. Use warm and cool colors of tissue paper.

1. Cut out squares of colored tissue paper. Separate the warm colors and the cool colors.

2. Overlap warm- and cool-colored tissue paper. Hold them up to the light. Then, overlap only warm and only cool colors.

Decide What happened when you overlapped warm and cool colors? Did the colors change when they were placed together?

Ester Stewart. Age 11. *Panic in the City.* Colored tissue paper and construction paper.

How do the colors and shapes of the artwork contribute to the mood?

Create

How can you create a specific mood in a collage? Use warm and cool colors to create a collage.

1. Think about the warm and cool colors you like.

2. Cut free-form and/or geometric shapes out of colored drawing paper and tissue paper.

3. Arrange your shapes. Combine the warm and cool colors. Allow the tissue paper to overlap some of the drawing paper colors. Glue your shapes onto the white background.

Describe What colors did you overlap? What shapes did you see?

Analyze Did you use warm and cool colors to organize your collage? Did changes occur when you overlapped colored areas with the tissue paper?

Interpret What mood was created by your use of colors?

Decide If you could do this over again, how would you make it different?

Visual Rhythm and Movement

Artists use visual rhythm and movement to add interest and visual excitement to artworks.

George McNeil. (American). *Deliverance Disco*. Montclair Art Museum, Montclair, New Jersey.

In *Deliverance Disco,* everything seems to be moving quickly. Observe how McNeil uses lines and color to express movement and add interest and excitement. The Egyptian wall fresco was created following strict rules. Certain parts of the body are drawn sideways. Other parts face forward. The artist used repetition to create visual movement. Both artists used different techniques to make our eyes move about the artwork as we observe it.

Unit 2

Artist unknown. (Egyptian). *Ipuy and his Wife receiving offerings from their children.* Fresco. 47.5 × 74 cm. Copy of wall painting from the tomb of Ipuy. Egyptian Expedition of the Metropolitan Museum of Art, New York, New York. Rogers Fund 1930.

Study both paintings to find examples of visual rhythm and movement.

✓ Where are lines or shapes that appear to move or flow?

✓ Where do your eyes look first in each painting and where do they look last? What causes this to happen?

✓ Which painting uses free-form shapes and which one uses geometric shapes?

✓ What feelings does each painting evoke?

SEEING LIKE AN ARTIST

Do you see repetition of lines, shapes, or colors in any objects around you? Where else have you seen repeated lines, shapes, or colors?

Lesson 5

63

Using Visual Rhythm and Movement

Visual Rhythm is a repeated pattern created by the repetition of shapes, color, or lines. It pulls the viewer's eyes through a work of art. **Pattern** is another word used to describe visual rhythm.

Movement means creating the illusion of movement through visual rhythm. Artists use movement to control the way a person looks at a work of art.

A **motif** is the object that is repeated or unit of objects that is repeated.

Five Types of Rhythm

 **Regular rhythm** occurs when each motif is repeated with the same amount of space between.

 **Alternate rhythm** repeats motifs but changes positions of the motifs or adds a second motif to the pattern.

 **Random rhythm** occurs when the motif is repeated in no apparent order.

 **Progressive rhythm** is a motif that changes each time it is repeated.

 **Flowing rhythm** is rhythm that repeats wavy lines.

Practice

Create designs using five types of visual rhythm. Use colored markers.

1. Fold paper into four sections. Label each section one of the five types of rhythm. Use the back of your paper and label one of your sections the last type of rhythm.

2. Think of a single design or motif. Repeat your design or motif to practice the five types of visual rhythm.

Decide Did you create the five kinds of visual rhythm? Did your designs create a sense of movement?

Unit **2**

Mandy Tomberlin. Age 9. *A Sunrise on the Mountain.* Dirt and glue.

What lines does the artist use to create a flowing rhythm?

Create

What rhythms do you see when you look at the landscape from your window? Create a landscape using flowing rhythm.

1. Think about the colors of the earth. Imagine using them to create a landscape.

2. Collect a variety of earth pigments. Grind your collected pigments. Add them to binder or glue.

3. Lightly draw a landscape using repeated curving lines to create a flowing rhythm.

4. Paint your landscape with the earth pigment paints. Experiment using different amounts of pigment and binder.

Describe How did you create some of your colors?

Analyze Did you use curved lines to create the feeling of flowing rhythm?

Interpret What mood did you create in your landscape?

Decide Were you successful in using flowing rhythm in your landscape?

Color and Visual Rhythm

Artists use color to express moods or feelings in their artworks.

Vincent van Gogh. (Dutch). *A Pair of Boots.* 1887. Oil on canvas. 13 × 16⅛ inches. Baltimore Museum of Art, Baltimore, Maryland. The Cone Collection, formed by Dr. Claribel Cone and Miss Etta Cone of Baltimore, Maryland.

How are these two paintings similar? Vincent van Gogh painted the shoes of a common man with dull colors to express the poverty that many people suffered. Jean-Étienne Liotard used bold colors to express the luxurious life of a rich woman. Both artists used colors to express certain moods and feelings in their paintings.

Jean-Étienne Liotard. (Swiss). *A Frankish Woman and Her Servant.* 1750. Oil on canvas. $28\frac{1}{2} \times 22\frac{1}{2}$ inches. Nelson-Atkins Museum of Art, Kansas City, Missouri. (Purchase Nelson Trust).

Think about how the artists use color to reveal the mood of each painting.

✓ What colors are used in both paintings?

✓ Which painting uses dull colors for the background?

✓ What mood or feeling is created in each painting?

✓ How does the artist's use of color affect the mood of each work?

SEEING LIKE AN ARTIST

What colors do your friends use to express themselves? How do you express yourself through color?

Lesson 6

Using Color and Visual Rhythm

A plan for organizing colors is called a **color scheme**. It is used to express a mood.

Visual rhythm is created by repeated shapes separated by the area around them. An artist can use rhythm to control the mood of an artwork.

Monochromatic color schemes use only one color and its tints and shades.

Analogous color schemes use colors that are side by side on the color wheel and have a common hue, such as yellow-green, yellow, yellow-orange, and orange.

Complementary colors cause visual excitement, and they are opposite each other on the color wheel.

Warm colors are red, yellow, and orange. They remind us of warm things and generally give us a feeling of energy.

Cool colors are blue, green, and violet. They are the opposite of warm colors.

Practice

Choose a color scheme to express your feelings. Use crayons.

1. Select a color scheme that best expresses who you are or how you are feeling.

2. With your selected color scheme, use crayons to draw lines or shapes to express your feelings.

Decide Did you use one color scheme to express your feelings?

Robert Landers. Age 11. *Rainbow over the Mountains.* Watercolors.

How do the colors and visual rhythms illustrate the mood and rhythm of music?

Create

What colors and visual rhythms can be used to express different moods? Use colors and visual rhythm to illustrate the mood of a piece of music.

1. Think about your favorite music. What emotions are being expressed in the music?

2. Create visual rhythm using different lines and shapes to illustrate the mood and rhythm of the music.

3. Select a color scheme that best represents the mood of the music. Fill the page with color.

Describe What was your color scheme? What lines and shapes did you draw?

Analyze How did you arrange your lines, shapes, and colors?

Interpret Does your work express the mood and rhythm of your music?

Decide Explain how the color scheme you chose affected the look of your work.

Rhythm in Dance

Rhapsody in Taps: *Eddie Brown with Linda Sohl-Donnell, Pauline Hagino and bass player.*

artists use color, lines, and shapes to create visual rhythm. Dancers like Eddie Brown use musical beats and their fast-flying feet to tap out rhythms in sound. Artists create moods and a sense of movement with repeated patterns of color, line, and shape. Tap dancers create moods with repeated patterns of movements and sounds.

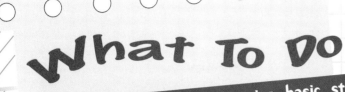

What To Do

Create rhythm patterns using basic steps.

Materials
- ✔ pencils
- ✔ paper

1. Make a list of different kinds of steps you do every day.

2. With a partner, take turns clapping out simple rhythmic patterns that your partner can echo. First, echo the rhythmic patterns with your hands, then with your feet.

3. Now try traveling as you make the rhythm patterns with your feet.

4. Sit in a circle with other students. Take turns going into the center and making some moves while everyone else claps the rhythm made by the feet of the solo dancer. Try to get different combinations of movements and rhythmic sounds.

Describe Describe the movements you used in your tap dances.

Analyze Explain how visual rhythms and sound rhythms are alike and different.

Interpret What mood did you create with rhythmic patterns?

Decide Were you more successful in creating rhythm patterns with your hands or with your feet?

Extra Credit ●●●●●●●●●●●●●●●●●●

Work out two or three rhythmic patterns that you can do with your feet. Put them in a sequence that includes doing each pattern twice. Perform for others.

Dance

Color, Rhythm, and Movement

Reviewing Main Ideas

The lessons and activities in Unit 2 cover the techniques that artists use to create color and visual rhythm.

- The **color spectrum** is the arrangement of colors seen when light passes through a prism. The **color wheel** is the spectrum bent into a circle. There are three sets of colors on the color wheel.

- **Hue** is another name for color. There are three groups of hues.

  1. **Primary** hues, or colors, are red, blue, and yellow.

  2. **Secondary** hues are violet, orange, and green. They are made by mixing together two primary hues.

  3. **Intermediate** hues are made by mixing a primary hue with the secondary hue next to it on the color wheel. Red-violet is an example.

- A **tint** is a light value of a hue made by adding white to it.

- A **shade** is a dark value of a hue that is made by adding black to it.

Peter Blume. (Russian). *Light of the World.* 1932. Oil on composition board. $18 \times 20\frac{1}{4}$ inches. Collection of Whitney Museum of American Art, New York. Purchase/Photography by Robert E. Mates, N.J. © 1998 Estate of Peter Blume/Licensed by VAGA, New York, NY.

- A **color scheme** is a plan for organizing colors.
  1. **Monochromatic** means only one color and its tints and shades.
  2. **Analogous** colors are side by side on the color wheel and share a common color.
  3. **Complementary** colors are opposite each other on the color wheel.
  4. **Warm** colors seem to move toward the viewer. They are red, yellow, and orange.
  5. **Cool** colors seem to move away from the viewer. They are blue, green, and violet.
- **Visual rhythm** is a repeated pattern of shapes, color, or line that creates a sense of movement.

Summing Up

In the painting *Light of the World,* Peter Blume used the techniques for creating color and visual rhythm covered in this unit.

- Look closely at the colors. What color scheme do you recognize? Is there more than one color scheme?
- Where do you see rhythm? Where is there regular rhythm?

Color and rhythm are both art elements used by artists to express a feeling or create visual excitement in a work of art. Color and rhythm are used in all kinds of art.

Careers in Art
Photographer

Richard Tichich is a photographer. There are two different kinds of photographers. Photojournalists are reporters who work for magazines and newspapers and tell stories through photographs. Fine art photographers work with studio, fashion, product and food, and nature photography. Tichich's parents were creative and took him to museums and galleries. He took many photography classes and obtained his graduate degree from the University of Texas at San Antonio. He says the best part about his work is that he can use both his creative and technical skills.

Richard Tichich, photographer

Unit 3

An Introduction to

Space, Form, and Texture

Artists use space, form, and texture in both two- and three-dimensional art forms.

Jan Vermeer. (Dutch). *Portrait of a Young Woman*. Oil on canvas. $17\frac{1}{2} \times 15\frac{3}{4}$ inches. Metropolitan Museum of Art, New York, New York.

Space is used by artists in paintings and drawings to give the illusion of depth on a flat surface.

- Notice the dark negative space around the figure. How did the artist use positive and negative space?

Artists use several techniques to create the illusion of **form** on a two-dimensional, or flat, surface.

- What did Vermeer do to make the figure look so realistic in this painting?

Artists sometimes suggest the **textures** of real objects.

- How did Vermeer suggest the textures of the fabrics and the person?

Artist Profile

Jan Vermeer
1632–1675

Jan Vermeer is an artist who was almost unknown until about a hundred years ago. He made fewer than 40 paintings and very little about his life was written. But those paintings show that he was one of the world's great artists. Vermeer was interested in how scenes of everyday life might look to a person who was standing a short distance away. He created for the viewer the textures, values, and shape and space relationships that natural light on a scene would show. Vermeer was only 43 years old when he died.

Like many artists, Jan Vermeer relied on the use of space, form, and texture to help him create realistic paintings. In this unit you will learn about the following topics:

- Space
- Form
- Types of Textures
- Architectural Form

Positive and Negative Space

**Artists use positive and negative spaces
to add interest to their artwork.**

Jasper Johns. (American).
Cups 4 Picasso. 1972.
Lithograph. $14\frac{1}{8} \times 32\frac{1}{4}$ inches.
Museum of Modern Art, New
York, New York. Licensed by
VAGA, New York. Gift of
Celeste Bartos.

Jasper Johns's lithographs are examples of optical
illusions. He has deliberately organized shapes to create
a visual puzzle to confuse the viewer. Johns likes to change a
recognizable object to attract more attention to it, as in the
way he changed the face of the Spanish artist Pablo Picasso.
Notice how Johns arranges shapes and uses color to add
interest to *Cups 4 Picasso*.

Jasper Johns. (American). *Cups 4 Picasso*. 1972.
Lithograph. $14\frac{1}{8} \times 32\frac{1}{4}$ inches. Museum of
Modern Art, New York, New York. Licensed by
VAGA, New York, Gift of Celeste Bartos.

Look closely at both views of *Cups 4 Picasso* by
Jasper Johns.

☑ What type of shapes do you see in both views?
Describe the area around each shape.

☑ How many shapes are in each view?

☑ What technique did Johns use to show us which shapes
are most important?

☑ What changes occur from one image to the next?

SEEING LIKE
AN ARTIST
Study a classmate's
face from the side.
What parts look
different from the side
than they do from the
front?

Using Positive and Negative Space

The element of art that refers to the area between, around, above, below, and within objects is **space**. Shapes and forms exist in space. It is the air around an object. There are two types of space—positive and negative.

Positive space is the objects, shapes, or forms in works of art.

Negative space is the empty space that surrounds objects, shapes, and forms. When there is a large area of negative space in an artwork, loneliness or freedom is expressed.

 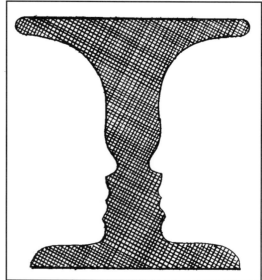

Shape reversal is when a shape or positive space starts out as one image and then in another image turns into the negative space. This is what happens in Johns's lithographs.

Practice

Practice drawing profiles. Use pencil.

1. Draw a profile of your partner's face.

2. Turn your paper upside down and copy the profile backwards just as Jasper Johns did.

Decide What does the negative space between the profiles look like?

Where is the negative space in the picture?

Elizabeth Armstrong. Age 10.
The Old Cane Chair. Marker, pencil.

Create

How can you see the shapes of negative space? Draw the negative shapes in a still life.

1. Think about objects for a still life that have large, interesting negative spaces, such as chairs or desks.

2. Look closely at the still life and find an area you like. Draw it, concentrating on the negative spaces around the objects.

3. Using markers, fill only the negative spaces with color. Leave the positive spaces white.

Describe Describe the positive shapes in your still-life drawing.

Analyze What shapes did you create when you colored the negative spaces? How do the positive and negative shapes differ?

Interpret How did reversing the positive and negative spaces affect your drawing?

Decide Do you like the way your still life turned out when you reversed the positive and negative spaces?

Positive and Negative Space Reversal

Artists sometimes use reverse positive and negative space to add imagination and movement to a piece of artwork.

M. C. Escher. (Dutch). *Sky and Water.* Woodcut. National Gallery of Art, Washington, DC.

Looking at Escher's artwork is like looking at an optical illusion. *Sky and Water* uses positive and negative space to change the water image to the sky image. Look only at the white shapes and then only at the black shapes. In *Reptiles,* his print draws the viewer's eye toward the reptile that is working its way out of the drawing. The reptiles move around the page, gradually changing from flat shapes to solid free-form forms.

M. C. Escher. (Dutch). *Reptiles*. 1943. Lithograph. $13\frac{1}{8}$ × 15 inches. National Gallery of Art, Washington, DC. Rosenwald Collection, © 1996 Board of Trustees.

Study both pieces of artwork to notice positive and negative space.

☑ Are there negative spaces in the middle of *Sky and Water*?

☑ How do the shapes, colors, and details change in *Sky and Water*?

☑ Where are the geometric shapes in *Reptiles*? How do they change into free-form shapes?

☑ How do the details of the reptiles change in this drawing?

SEEING LIKE AN ARTIST

Can you find positive and negative space in the artwork in your classroom?

Using Progressive Reversal

When an object starts out as one object or form and slowly changes into another object or form, it is called **progressive reversal**. This is also known as *progressive rhythm* because it gives the illusion of moving from one image to another.

Progressive means to change or move forward. In progressive reversal, there is a very slow change from one object to another. The object may slowly change size, shape, or color.

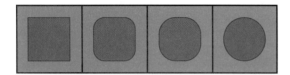

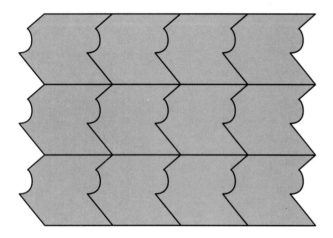

Unlike progressive reversal, which changes gradually, **tessellations** are a type of shape reversal that changes quickly and fits together like a puzzle.

Practice

Create a design using progressive change. Use black marker.

1. Divide your paper into five boxes. Begin by drawing a square in the first box and a circle in the fifth box.

2. Begin to slowly change your square shape into the circle in each of the boxes.

Decide How did you change your image from a square to a circle?

Paula Kramer. Age 11. *Design.* Markers.

Which shapes are positive and which are negative in the tessellation puzzle design?

Create

What kind of puzzle would you like to design? Create a tessellation puzzle design using positive and negative shapes.

1. Think about how the shapes of a puzzle fit together. Draw a perfect square.

2. Cut out a shape from one edge of a square. Tape it onto the opposite edge of the square.

3. Trace around the new shape, locking shapes together like pieces of a puzzle. See the example below.

4. Use color to create a pattern.

Describe Describe the shapes you created. List the steps you followed.

Analyze How does positive and negative space work in your tessellation?

Interpret How do you feel about making a design like this?

Decide Did you successfully create a tessellation design?

Square

Cut shape from paper.

Tape it to opposite side.

Texture

Designers combine a variety of textures to make exterior
and interior spaces interesting and appealing.

Artist unknown. (England) *Caravan* (Outside view). Built 1915. John Pocketts,
owner. From *English Style* by Suzanne Slesin & Stafford Cliff. Reprinted by
permission of Clarkson N. Potter, a division of Crown Publishers, Inc.

A caravan is a large covered vehicle, like a wagon or a
home on wheels. The builders used repeated
shapes and lines on the outside of the caravan to create
interest. Some areas look rough, while others look smooth.
The interior, or inside, of the caravan is a combination of
materials. Each surface or material has a different feel.
Some look smooth and shiny, while others look bumpy.

Artist unknown. (England) *Caravan* (End view). Built 1915. John Pocketts, owner. From *English Style* by Suzanne Slesin & Stafford Cliff. Reprinted by permission of Clarkson N. Potter, a division of Crown Publishers, Inc.

Look closely at both photographs. Notice how texture is used.

☑ Where do you see a twisted, bumpy surface?

☑ Which areas look smooth or shiny?

☑ Where do you see repeated shapes or lines? What type of feel do they create?

☑ What are some similarities and differences between the materials used on the outside and those used on the inside?

SEEING LIKE AN ARTIST
Think of all the objects and materials that decorate your room. How do these different objects feel?

Using Texture in Interior Spaces

Texture is the element of art that refers to how things feel, or look as if they might feel if touched. There are two ways in which we experience texture—by sight or by touch.

Tactile texture is texture that you feel.

Visual texture is the way something looks like it might feel if you could touch it. It is the illusion an artist creates to represent texture. A rubbing is one way to show visual texture. Other examples of visual texture are examples you see in magazines.

Imitated textures are also two-dimensional. They imitate real textures. When you look at the textures in a photograph, they are imitated textures.

Practice

Create some visual textures. Use crayons.

1. To record textures, create rubbings of them.

2. Choose some raised textures, like the soles of a sneaker. Place a thin sheet of paper over each texture to be rubbed. Use the flat side of a crayon while holding the paper in place. Rub the flat side of a crayon over the paper away from your fingers in one direction.

Decide What textures transferred best?

Vanesa Garcia. Age 11. *Clubhouse.* Magazines.

What textures do you see in the picture?

Create

What textures would you use to design the interior of a clubhouse? Create a collage of the inside of a fantasy clubhouse using visual textures.

1. Think about creating the inside of a fantasy clubhouse. Choose an idea for a theme.

2. Draw several quick sketches of the inside. Choose one sketch to reproduce. Concentrate on the main shapes.

3. Collect a variety of visual textures, like the texture of frosting or a shiny car. Cut out, then arrange and glue your textures onto your drawing.

Describe Describe the textures and objects in your clubhouse.

Analyze Do the textures you collected copy textures of real objects?

Interpret What kind of mood does your clubhouse have? Is it a quiet space or a space for fun?

Decide What other pictures can be created using this collage technique?

Architectural Form and Texture

Artists often use shading techniques to create the illusion
of form and texture on a two-dimensional surface.

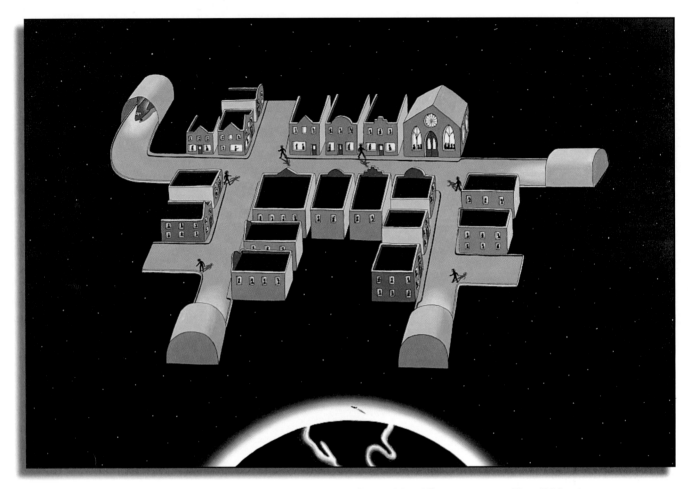

Roger Brown. (American). *Homesick Proof Space Station.* 1987. Oil on canvas. 48 × 72 inches.
Courtesy of the Phyllis Kind Gallery.

The painting *Homesick Proof Space Station,* done in 1987, actually makes fun of space travel. The artist is being sarcastic. *Space Station #1* by Robert McCall was created for the MGM movie *2001: A Space Odyssey* in the 1970s. What familiar shapes do you find in the artworks?

Robert McCall. (American). *Space Station #1*. Mixed media on canvas. $53 \times 40\frac{1}{2}$ inches. Commissioned by MGM for the film *2001: A Space Odyssey*. National Museum of Air and Space, Smithsonian Institution, Washington, DC.

Study both paintings to find textures and forms.

✓ Find a smooth, shiny surface and a rough surface.

✓ Find a cylinder or cube. Are there overlapping forms?

✓ What effect does it have on the subject when an object goes from light to dark?

✓ What was done to create the feeling of floating in space?

SEEING LIKE AN ARTIST
Look around you for shapes similar to the objects in these two paintings.

Shading to Create Architectural Form and Texture

A **form** is any object that can be measured in three ways: height, width, and depth. In two-dimensional art, artists create the illusion of form using various techniques. They also use shading techniques to create a different quality of texture.

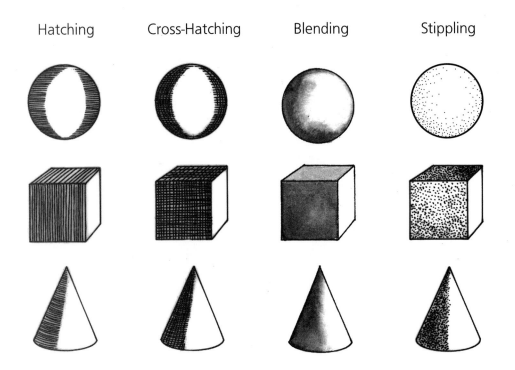

Hatching   Cross-Hatching   Blending   Stippling

To create the illusion of form on a two-dimensional surface, artists use imitated textures. Textures can be used to change a shape into a form.

Practice

Change shapes into forms by using different types of shading techniques. Use pencil.

1. Lightly draw four different shapes. Beneath each, write *hatching, cross-hatching, stippling, or blending.*

2. Change each shape into a form using the shading technique written below it.

Decide Which technique did you like best?

Mike Kwon. Age 11. *Silent Steel*. Oil pastel.

How do the shading techniques affect the appearance of the space station?

Create

What types of forms would you use to design your own space station? Draw a three-dimensional space station using shading techniques to create the illusion of texture and form.

1. Think about how both artists used shading techniques to create forms on a flat surface.

2. Sketch your space station using simple shapes. Use the shading techniques to change these shapes into forms.

3. Draw planets using the blending technique to move from light to dark. Try complementary colors for shading. Add white highlights.

4. Add atmosphere by using the side of the oil pastel to make long sweeping marks.

Describe Describe your space station and the shapes you used to build it.

Analyze What shading techniques did you use?

Interpret How did the colors and textures affect the appearance of your station? Would you like to live there?

Decide If you could make another space station, what would you do to improve it?

Architectural Shape and Visual Texture

Architects are artists who design buildings and structures for living, working, and leisure.

Elizabeth Plater-Zyberk. (American). *Seaside, Florida, Walkway*. Architecture. Courtesy of Andres Duany and Elizabeth Plater-Zyberk.

Elizabeth Plater-Zyberk designed this group of houses and walkways in the 1980s. Her structures remind us of the pastel sunsets found near the ocean. Architect Frank Lloyd Wright designed homes that were primarily built to blend with their environments. Notice the materials used for the structures by the two architects.

Frank Lloyd Wright. (American).
Fallingwater. Bear Run, Pennsylvania,
1936–1939. Glen Allison/Tony Stone Images
© 1998 © 1996 Artists Rights Society (ARS),
NY/Frank Lloyd Wright Foundation.

Study both photographs to find architectural shapes.

☑ Find the geometric and free-form shapes.

☑ Where are the windows, doors, and roofs?

☑ Do the architectural shapes blend in with the
environments that surround them? If so, how?

SEEING LIKE
AN ARTIST
What types of details
do the homes and
buildings in your
community have? Do
they have unusual
windows, roofs, or
doors?

Using Architectural Shapes

Architecture is the art of designing and planning the construction of buildings, cities, and bridges. An **architect** is a person who plans and designs buildings, cities, and bridges.

Types of Architectural Shapes

Practice

Practice drawing some of the architectural shapes you have learned about. Use pencil.

1. Lightly sketch the overall shape of a building or house you have seen. Include an environment.

2. Add architectural shapes to your sketch. Keep the basic structure of your original drawing.

Decide What architectural shapes did you draw?

Liliana Jimenez. Age 11. *Town and Country*. Crayons, marker.

What architectural shapes do you see in the picture?

Create

What types of architectural detail does your home have? Draw the building you live in using architectural shapes.

1. Think about the architectural shapes and details in your community. Lightly sketch with pencil the main shapes of the building where you live.

2. Draw architectural shapes such as windows, doors, roofs, and the surrounding environment.

3. Using a black felt-tip pen, outline your drawing. Complete your drawing with colored pencils, adding details.

Describe Describe the shapes and forms used.

Analyze What types of architectural shapes are in your drawing?

Interpret How do the colors, textures, and architectural shapes affect the mood of the drawing?

Decide Could you use these techniques to draw an imaginary building?

Form and Tactile Texture

Artists use form to create three-dimensional
works of art.

Le Corbusier. (Swiss). *Chapelle de Notre-Dame du Haut.* 1950–55. Ronchamp, France.
Girandon/Art Resource, NY © 1998 Artists Rights Society (ARS), NY/ADAGP, Paris/FLC.

Le Corbusier was an architect who created *Chapelle
de Notre-Dame du Haut* in France in 1950. *The Sydney
Opera House* in Sydney, Australia, was designed in 1957 by
Jorn Utzon of Denmark. Do you think these structures
resemble a chapel and an opera house? Both architects used
shapes found in nature as a basis for their designs.

Unit 3

Jørn Oberg Utzon. (Danish). *Opera House.* Sydney, Australia.

Study both architectural structures for their use of form and texture.

- ✓ What two shapes and forms do you see in both structures?

- ✓ What is unique about these two buildings?

- ✓ Do you think both structures fit their environments? Why?

SEEING LIKE AN ARTIST

What objects can you think of that are similar to the structures in the photographs?

Using Form and Tactile Texture

A **form** is an object that is three-dimensional. Like a shape, a form has length and width, but it also has depth. Forms can be either geometric or free-form. You must view forms from all angles to truly understand them.

Armatures are frameworks for supporting material used in sculpting, such as clay. An armature helps hold the material up and in place.

Tactile texture is an actual texture that you can touch and feel. The way light reflects off the surface of an object depends on the texture of that object.

 **Rough**-textured surfaces reflect the light unevenly.

 **Smooth**-textured surfaces reflect the light evenly.

 **Shiny**-textured surfaces reflect a bright light.

 **Matte**-textured surfaces reflect a light that is soft with an almost dull look.

Practice

Find objects with combinations of textures.

1. Working in small groups, find textures in your surroundings.

2. Find rough and shiny, then rough and matte-finished. Find smooth and shiny, then smooth and matte.

Decide Do you understand the many combinations of textures?

Dung Tran. Rudy Espino. Lenny Rodriguez. *Clay Houses.* Clay, paint.

What do you think the purpose of the buildings is?

Create

What is your favorite kind of public building? Build a clay model of a unique public building.

1. Think about a building for your favorite activities. Begin creating it by taping together small boxes or wads of newspaper for an armature. Make clay slabs for the walls and roof.

2. Put your building together. Use proper clay-joining techniques to build your structure. (See page 204.)

3. Add details such as windows and doors by adding clay or carving openings. Use found materials to create textures on the clay surface.

Describe What kind of a unique building did you create? Explain how you created the forms and textures.

Analyze Describe the forms and textures you used.

Interpret Does your building look like its function? Give it a name.

Decide Were you able to control the slabs to create the forms you planned?

Space, Form, and Texture in Music

Xochimoki: *Jim Berenholtz and Mazatl Galindo.*

These musicians use musical instruments like those played by ancient Aztec and Mayan peoples. They make music with things like a log drum, a gourd trumpet, rattles made of seeds, and a turtle shell drum played with deer antlers. Artists use the forms of nature as the basis for their designs. These musicians use the materials of nature as the basis for their music.

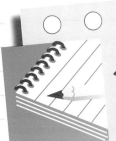

What To Do

Write a musical score.

Materials
- ✔ paper and pencils
- ✔ found sources of sound

1. Collect common items that create sound. These sound sources will be your classroom collection of instruments.

2. Classify the instruments as to how you make sound with them. Are they shaken, blown, scraped, or struck? On a large chart draw a descriptive symbol for each category. For example, you could draw a simple horn for instruments that are blown and a rattle for those that are shaken.

3. Form a class orchestra, grouping the instruments into their categories. Set a beat by tapping your feet. Then, play your instruments together.

4. Write a musical score using your symbols so that another group could perform your work.

Describe Describe the instruments you created.

Analyze How is your use of nature's materials similar to an artist's use of nature's designs?

Interpret What feelings and moods did you create?

Decide How well do you think you succeeded in creating music? What did you like best about this activity?

Extra Credit

Decorate your musical score in an artistic way, mount it on colorful paper, and display it with a description.

Space, Form, and Texture

Reviewing Main Ideas

The activities and lessons in this unit cover space, form, and texture and how they are used by artists to create works of art.

- **Space**—The element of art that refers to the area between, around, above, below, and within objects. There are two types of space.

1. **Positive space** is the objects, shapes, or forms in all works of art.

2. **Negative space** is the empty space that surrounds objects, shapes, or forms.

- **Texture** is the element of art that refers to how things feel, or look as if they might feel if touched. There are two ways in which we experience texture.

1. **Visual texture** is the way something looks like it might feel if you could touch it. There are two types of visual texture.

a. **Invented textures** are two-dimensional patterns created by repetition of shapes and lines.

b. **Simulated textures** are two-dimensional patterns that imitate real textures.

2. **Tactile texture** is an actual texture. You can touch it and feel it.

Alexander Calder. (American). *Untitled Mobile*. 1976. Aluminum and steel. $358\frac{1}{2}$ × $911\frac{1}{2}$ inches. National Gallery of Art, Washington, DC. Gift of the Collectors' Committees, © 1996 Board of Trustees, National Gallery of Art, Washington, DC. Photo by Philip A. Charles.

- **Form** is any object that can be measured in three ways: height, width, and depth.
- **Architectural Forms** are the shapes and structures that relate to the rules of architecture.

Summing Up

Look at *Untitled Mobile* by Alexander Calder. The artist thought carefully about space, form, and texture when he created his mobiles. Several of these techniques were discussed in Unit 3.

- Has Alexander Calder used both types of space in his mobile?
- What basic shapes did Calder use? Why is this mobile considered an example of a three-dimensional form?
- Describe the textures used by Calder. Are they simulated, or tactile?

Space, form, and texture create the illusion of depth on two-dimensional works of art and make three-dimensional works more interesting for the viewer.

Let's Visit a Museum

The National Gallery of Art in Washington, DC, was built for the people of the United States. Upon his death, Andrew W. Mellon, the financier, donated money and his art collection to create the museum. It opened in 1941. The major collection includes more than 100,000 sculptures, paintings, drawings, decorative objects, prints, and photographs. Because the National Gallery of Art was built to give all people access to a museum, there are no admission fees.

The National Gallery of Art

Unit 4

An Introduction to

Proportion and Distortion

Proportion and distortion are used by artists in both sculptural forms and pictures.

Frida Kahlo. (Mexican). *Frieda and Diego, Wedding Portrait.* 1931. Oil on canvas. $39\frac{3}{8} \times 31$ inches. San Francisco Museum of Modern Art, San Francisco, California. Albert M. Bender Collection, gift of Albert M. Bender. Photo by Ben Blackwell.

Artists use several techniques to create **proportion** in a work of art.

- How does Kahlo use the clothing to increase size? What effect do the full dress and shawl have? How do the hands compare to the size of the palette?

- How tall do you think Frida Kahlo was? To what are you comparing her to get an idea of her height?

Distortion is used by artists in paintings and drawings to express a feeling or idea.

- What message about the relationship of the two figures was Kahlo trying to convey in this painting?

Artist Profile

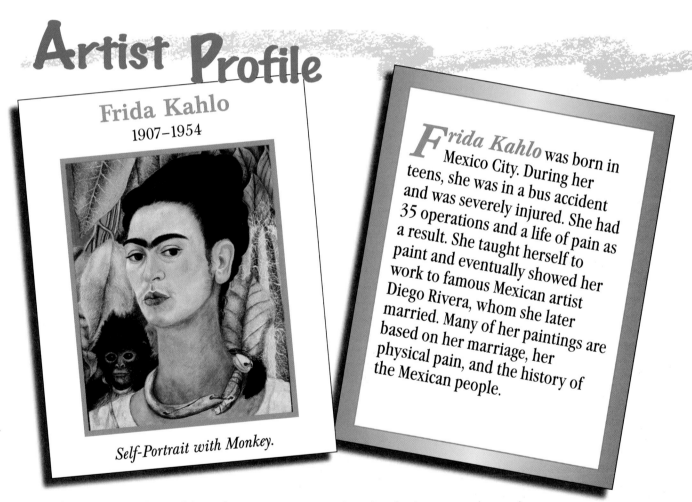

Frida Kahlo
1907–1954

Self-Portrait with Monkey.

Frida Kahlo was born in Mexico City. During her teens, she was in a bus accident and was severely injured. She had 35 operations and a life of pain as a result. She taught herself to paint and eventually showed her work to famous Mexican artist Diego Rivera, whom she later married. Many of her paintings are based on her marriage, her physical pain, and the history of the Mexican people.

Artists like Frida Kahlo often use proportion in their artwork to show relative sizes and to imitate realism. Other artists choose to use distortion in their artwork to convey a feeling or thought. Unit 4 focuses on the following topics:

- Proportion
- Scale
- Distortion
- Exaggeration

Proportion

Artists use proportion to show how people or things relate to one another in size.

Hubert Robert. (French). *The Artist Drawing a Young Girl*. 1773. Red chalk on paper. 25.5 cm × 33.8 cm. Metropolitan Museum of Art, New York, New York. Bequest of Walter C. Baker, 1971.

Hubert Robert created *The Artist Drawing a Young Girl*. French artists of the eighteenth century painted portraits of wealthy people enjoying life and having fun. *Don Manuel Osorio Manrique de Zuniga* was painted by Francisco Goya. Goya was well known for his portraits of aristocrats. Each artist uses proportion to show the size of the child.

Francisco Goya. (Spanish). *Don Manuel Osorio Manrique de Zuniga.* 1784. Metropolitan Museum of Art, New York, New York.

Study both works of art to notice the proportion.

✓ What ages do you think the girl and boy are in both works of art?

✓ How tall do you think they are? What clues in the pictures tell you how tall they are?

✓ Describe the differences in size between the little girl, the man drawing her, and the woman watching the scene.

SEEING LIKE AN ARTIST
Compare the sizes of your classmates to the objects around them. What are some of your observations?

Using Proportion

Proportion is the principle of art concerned with the size relationships of one part to another such as a hand to a wrist. Artists use several techniques to draw things in proportion.

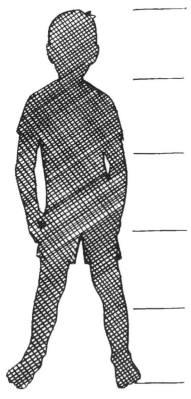

Average Body Proportions
of 10 year old.

Body Proportions:
Although people vary in size and shape, most people have the same proportions. Artists use the length of the head, from the chin to the top of the skull, to help them in measuring proportion. A child may be five heads long while an infant might be only three heads long.

Practice

Measure body proportions. Use string.

1. With a string, measure a partner's head from the top of the skull to the bottom of the chin. Using the length of the head as a unit of measurement, measure the rest of the body. For example, the length of an arm might be two head lengths.

2. Record and compare your findings.

Decide What did you learn about proportion by doing this activity?

Andrew Williams. Age 11. *My Friend Al.* Oil pastel.

How many heads tall is the boy in the artwork? How old do you think he is?

Create

How can you use the sighting technique to draw a person in proportion? Sketch a model, using the sighting technique to determine proportion.

1. Think about proportion as it relates to people. Looking at a class model, use the sighting technique to determine the proportions of the model.

2. Lightly sketch the basic body parts of the model using a light color. Oil pastels cover the color beneath them.

3. Fill your paper with colors.

Describe Describe the colors, lines, and shapes you used.

Analyze How did you place your lines using the sighting technique?

Interpret What is the mood of your finished work?

Decide Were you able to successfully use the sighting technique to draw the model in proportion?

Scale

Artists use scale to relate one object to
another in a work of art.

Domenico Ghirlandaio. (Italian).
Francesco Sasetti and His Son Teodoro.
c. 1480. Tempera on wood. $29\frac{1}{2} \times 20\frac{1}{2}$
inches. The Metropolitan Museum of Art,
New York, New York. The Jules Bache
Collection, 1949.

Ghirlandaio was best known for his portraits
during a period in history called the Renaissance.
He often included architecture in his paintings to create
the illusion of space. Nanha painted during the Mughal
period of art in India. His subject, the Emperor Shah
Jahan, built the Taj Mahal. Notice how differently each
father is interacting with his son. What does this tell you
about each relationship? Notice how both artists use
scale to relate one subject to another.

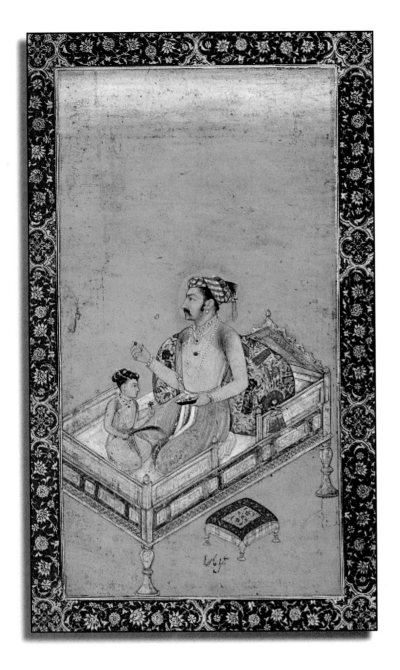

Nanha the Mughal. (Indian). *Emperor Shah Jahan and His Son, Suja.* 1625–30. Colors on gilt on paper. $15\frac{5}{16} \times 10\frac{5}{16}$ inches. Metropolitan Museum of Art, New York, New York. Purchase, Rogers Fund and The Kevorkian Foundation Gift, 1955.

Study both paintings to learn about scale.

✓ How big are the people in both works of art? What clues suggest their sizes?

✓ If the bed were not in Nanha the Mughal's painting, how would you be able to tell the sizes of the people?

✓ Do you see anything unusual about the child in one of the paintings in relation to his father?

✓ As a viewer, where are you in relation to each picture? How does this affect the way you see the people in these paintings?

Lesson 2

SEEING LIKE AN ARTIST

How can you show an object in a drawing so that someone looking at it will know how big that object is?

Using Scale

Scale is similar to proportion in that it deals with size relationships. The difference is that scale refers to size as measured against a standard reference, like the human body. Scale can be created realistically or unrealistically.

Realistic Scale: When an artist creates a work of art where everything seems to fit together and make sense in size relation, it is called realistic scale.

Unrealistic Scale: When an artist makes size relationships that do not make sense, the scale becomes unrealistic. Making a small object, such as a coin, larger than the hand holding it creates unrealistic scale.

Practice

Practice drawing an object using realistic scale. Use pencil.

1. Draw your hand to create an object of standard size.

2. Select an object that is either larger or smaller than your hand. Draw the object in scale to your hand. The entire object may not fit on your paper.

Decide What are some other ways to create realistic scale?

Marcia Saunders. Age 10. *Cars and Kids*. Collage.

What kind of scale did the artist use in her collage?

Create

How can you make a point through your artwork using unrealistic scale? Create a collage using unrealistic scale.

1. Think about objects and an indoor or outdoor background to use in your collage. Cut out pictures of objects, some that are in proper scale and one or two images that are too large or too small for the other objects.

2. Arrange your collected images so that they overlap and touch the edges of your paper. Keep the arrangement organized so that it is almost realistic.

3. Glue down the background. Next, glue the remaining objects. Make sure that at least one object shows unrealistic scale.

Describe Describe the objects you selected for your collage.

Analyze How are the objects arranged to create unrealistic scale?

Interpret Does your collage convey humor?

Decide Do you feel you were able to clearly portray unrealistic scale in an organized manner?

Facial Proportions

Artists use proportion to help them correctly organize
the features of a face.

Raphael. (Italian). *Bindo Altoviti.*
c. 1515. Oil on panel. $23\frac{1}{2} \times 17\frac{1}{4}$
inches. National Gallery of Art,
Washington, DC. Samuel H.
Kress Collection.

Raphael's paintings have the sculptural quality of
Michelangelo, the grace and feeling of Leonardo
da Vinci, and the detail of his first teacher, Perugino. Renoir
was interested in the bright and cheerful effect of light and
air, which was typical of his style of painting. His interest was
in painting people in pleasant surroundings. Both artists
painted portraits with character and expression.

Pierre Auguste Renoir.
(French). *Marguerite (Margot)*
Bérard. 1879. Oil on canvas.
$16\frac{1}{8} \times 12\frac{3}{4}$ inches.
Metropolitan Museum of Art,
New York, New York. Bequest
of Stephen C. Clark, 1960.

Study both paintings to understand facial proportions.

✓ What is the difference in the position of each face?

✓ How does the eye look different in a side view
compared to a front view? How does the mouth look
different?

✓ Where are the ears in relation to the eyes and nose?

✓ What differences do you notice in the features of the
child compared with those of the young man?

**SEEING LIKE
AN ARTIST**

Observe the
differences in side
views and front views
of your classmates.
Notice how their
features change.

Using Facial Proportions

Artists use **facial proportions** to help place features correctly on the human face. Lines, lightly drawn on a shape, are guidelines used by the artist to draw both full-face and profile portraits more accurately.

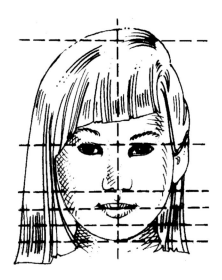

Facial Proportions:
A front view of the head can be divided by drawing three horizontal lines across a vertical center line called the **central axis**. In the example, notice how the eyes are drawn on the center line, the lips just below the bottom line, and the ears between the center and lower horizontal lines. The nose is above the bottom line on the central axis. The hairline is near the top line.

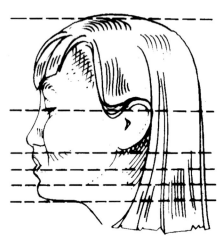

Profile Proportions: When you view a head in profile, or side view, all the horizontal proportion lines remain the same as in the front view. The shape of the head and the shapes of the features change. Notice the space between the eye and the ear and the chin. Notice that the shape of the head in the profile is different from the front view.

Practice

Practice drawing a profile. Use pencil.

1. Draw the shape of the head in profile. Add guidelines, using the second drawing shown above as a reference.

2. Add eyes, nose, mouth, chin, ear, hair, and neck.

Decide Were you able to create a profile using guidelines?

Where is the central axis of this portrait?

Chad Keeling. Age 10. *Myron.* Pencil.

Create

What is the best way to draw features on a portrait? Working with a partner, draw a portrait using facial proportions.

1. Think about the shape and size of your partner's head.

2. Measure the size of your partner's head. Mark off the dimensions on paper. Next, lightly draw guidelines for the eyes.

3. Use shading to draw hair, eyebrows, and clothing. Also use it to draw around the neck and shoulders and to add shadows to the skin.

Describe Describe the shapes and lines used to draw the features in your portrait.

Analyze How can this technique of drawing portraits be used to draw anyone?

Interpret What does the person in your portrait seem to be thinking?

Decide Were you successful in getting the features of your portrait in proportion? What would you do to make it better?

Exaggeration

Artists sometimes use exaggeration rather than real proportion to express their ideas or feelings.

Fernando Botero. (Colombian). *Ruben's Wife.* 1963. Oil on canvas. $72\frac{1}{8} \times 70\frac{1}{8}$ inches. Guggenheim Museum, New York, New York. Photograph by David Heald © The Solomon R. Guggenheim Foundation, New York.

Fernando Botero is best known for giving all his models plump proportions that he calls "plasticity." This creates a whimsical mood. Modigliani painted extended figures with few details, which creates a feeling of elegance. Both artists used exaggeration.

Amedeo Modigliani. (Italian). *Portrait of a Polish Woman.* 1918. Oil on canvas. $39\frac{1}{2} \times 25\frac{1}{2}$ inches. Philadelphia Museum of Art, Philadelphia, Pennsylvania. The Louis E. Stern Collection. Photo by Graydon Wood, 1994.

Study the paintings on these pages to find exaggeration.

☑ Where do you see a lengthened or stretched figure? A figure that is puffed up?

☑ What are some descriptive words to explain what these artists have done to the people in their paintings?

☑ Why do you think the artists changed the figures in this way?

☑ What emotional qualities do these figures suggest to you?

SEEING LIKE AN ARTIST

Look in books and newspapers to find examples of exaggeration.

Using Exaggeration

Exaggeration is a change from expected normal proportion by increasing part or all of a person or object. Some artists use exaggeration rather than accurate proportion to express strong feelings and ideas.

Exaggeration occurs in drawings, paintings, and even in sculptures. Artists can lengthen, enlarge, or bend parts of the body. By making these changes, they can show moods and feelings that are easy to understand.

Practice

From a newspaper, collect editorial cartoons featuring a politician.

1. Look through your newspaper for an editorial cartoon of a politician. Next, find a photo of that same politician.

2. Compare the exaggerated features of the person in the cartoon with his or her features in the photo.

Decide Why was the feature exaggerated by the cartoonist? What effect did that exaggeration have?

Chad Ethridge. Age 10. *Wolfman and Jupiter Man.* Markers.

What parts did the artist exaggerate?

Create

What kind of a character would you create if you were a cartoonist? Create an original comic strip character using exaggeration.

1. Think about comic strip characters you see every day. Then, draw several sketches of your own original comic strip character.

2. Choose one sketch. Exaggerate one or more features to show whether the character is funny, an action character, a superhero, or a fantasy creature. Give your character a name.

Describe Describe the features you exaggerated on your character.

Analyze Explain how you decided which feature to exaggerate and how you exaggerated that feature.

Interpret What emotional qualities does your character show?

Decide Do you like the way the exaggerated feature changed the mood of your drawing? Explain.

Distortion

Distortion is used by artists to create an expressive effect in a work of art.

Artist unknown. Tlingit (Alaska). *Dead-man Mask.* Nineteenth century. Wood, paint, hide metal. $13\frac{5}{8}$ inches high. Metropolitan Museum of Art, New York, New York.

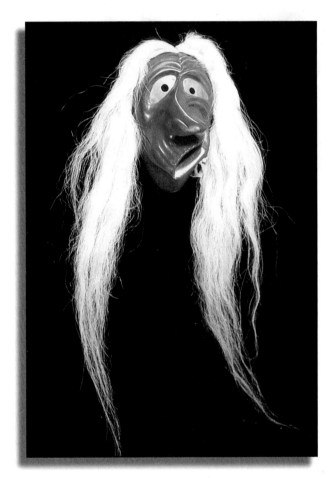

Elon Webster. Iroquois. *False Face Mask.* 1937. Wood. Cranbrook Institute of Science, Bloomfield Hills, Michigan.

Masks are used in many cultures as part of religious ceremonies and rituals. In many cases, the facial features of the masks are distorted for expressive purposes. Each culture has its own traditions and procedures for making and using masks. Sometimes the mask appears to a person in a dream. Often, the mask is part of a cultural tradition. In most cases, the mask is intended to help humans communicate with the spirit world.

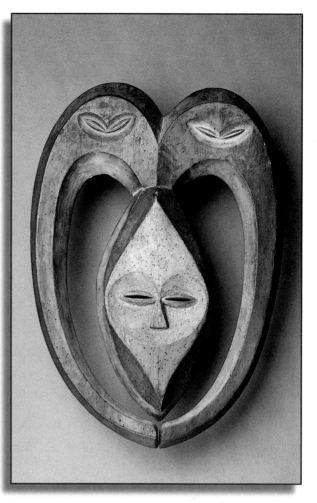

Artist unknown. Tlaticlo Valley of Mexico. *Mask.* 12th–9th century B.C. Ceramic pigment. $5\frac{1}{4}$ inches high. Metropolitan Museum of Art, New York, New York.

Artist unknown. Gabon or Congo (Kwele). *Kwele Face Mask.* 19th–20th century. Wood, paint. $20\frac{3}{4}$ inches tall. (52.7 cm) The Metropolitan Museum of Art, The Michael C. Rockefeller Memorial Collection, Bequest of Nelson A. Rockefeller, 1979. (1979.206.8) Photograph © 1986 The Metropolitan Museum of Art.

Study the four masks to learn more about distortion.

☑ Which mask shows the most distortion? Which shows the least?

☑ Use one adjective to describe the expressive quality of each mask.

☑ Use your imagination to figure out the purpose of each mask.

☑ What do all four masks have in common? What are their differences?

SEEING LIKE AN ARTIST

Think of different ways masks are used today. What are some ways that artists have changed masks to suit special occasions?

Using Distortion

Distortion is a change from expected normal proportions. Artists can distort a figure by bending, warping, stretching, squashing, or twisting it. Artists use distortion in paintings, drawings, and sculptures.

Practice

Design a mask. Use pencil.

1. Design a mask that will address a problem you are interested in such as poverty or crime. Make sketches of your mask.

2. Distort the features of the mask to emphasize the problem you are addressing.

Decide Did you create some good sketches? What features did you distort?

What did the artist distort in her mask?

Deidre. Age 11. *Mask*. Papier-mâché and tempera.

Create

How does a mask express a certain feeling or idea? Create a distorted papier-mâché mask.

1. Think what you want your mask to look like. Tear strips of newspaper 1 inch wide. Dip strips into the paste and wipe off excess liquid. Lay the strips over the outside of a plastic milk container. Overlap two layers of newspaper.

2. Dry the base, then add the features. Tape the shapes onto the base. Distort the features. Apply two more layers of papier-mâché, and let the mask base dry overnight.

3. When it is dry, pop your mask off the container and trim the edges. Paint the mask and apply other objects.

Describe Describe the shapes, colors, and textures of your mask.

Analyze How did you distort the features on your mask?

Interpret What feelings does your mask suggest? Which parts affect the feeling most?

Decide Were you successful in creating a distorted mask that expressed a certain feeling or idea?

Lesson 5

Scale and Proportion

Artists use proportion and scale to create life-size
sculptures and place them in realistic settings.

George Segal/Licensed by VAGA,
New York, NY. (American). *Walk Don't Walk*.
1976. Plaster, cement, metal, painted wood
and electric light. 104 × 72 × 72 inches.
Whitney Museum of American Art,
New York, New York.

Segal began his career as a painter but then turned
to creating life-size sculptures by covering casts of
people with gauze-embedded plaster. Hanson produced
lifelike sculptures and dressed them in real clothes. They were
so realistic they were mistaken for live people. Both artists
placed their life-size figures in settings with realistic objects
from everyday life.

Duane Hanson. (American). *Football Player.* 1981. Oil on polyvinyl. $43\frac{1}{4}$ x 30 x $31\frac{1}{2}$ inches. Museum purchase through funds from the Friends of Art and public subscriptions, 82.0024. © Lowe Art Museum, University of Miami, all rights reserved.

Study both sculptures to find realistic and lifelike things.

- ✓ Which artist's work looks more realistic? Explain.

- ✓ What are the people doing in each sculpture?

- ✓ Why did the artists include real objects with their sculptures?

- ✓ Can you figure out which objects in each work were not created by the sculptor but were added?

SEEING LIKE AN ARTIST

If they were creating sculptures to place within your school, what activities do you think these artists would represent?

Lesson 6

Using Scale and Proportion

Body proportions are defined in ratios of one part of the body to another.

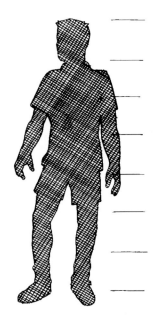

A **ratio** is a comparison of size between two things. Often artists will use the head as a ratio of one to the length of an adult body, which is about seven and a half head lengths. Therefore, the ratio would be 1 (the head) to 7 (heads per body length) and be written as 1:7.

Scale is similar to proportion in that it deals with size relationships. The difference is that scale refers to size as measured against a standard reference, like the human body.

Practice

Find examples of scale and proportion.

1. Divide into small groups. Think of a scene that Hanson or Segal might create. Collect props that are either in scale or out of scale to your body proportions.

2. Set up your living sculpture for the class to see.

Decide Do your classmates recognize whether you are working in scale or out of scale with your objects?

Fort Daniel Elementary fifth-grade class. *Life-size Sculpture.*
Clothes, pantyhose, newspaper.

How can you tell scale and proportion were used?

Create

What effect would a life-size sculpture have if you placed it somewhere in the school? Create a life-size figure using scale and proportion. Place it in a real environment in your school.

1. Think about available items you have to make a life-size soft sculpture. Work in small groups. Plan and make sketches of your figure and environment.

2. Divide responsibilities. Some can create the soft sculpture head. Others can stuff clothes with newspapers. Others can construct the environment. Make sure your figure is in scale with the environment.

3. Make a sign showing the title of the work.

Describe Describe the materials used to create your sculpture and environment.

Analyze Whom does your character represent? What is the setting of your sculpture?

Interpret What is the mood of your sculpture? What are observers likely to think your sculpture represents?

Decide Were you successful in creating a life-size sculpture that is in realistic scale and proportion?

Lesson 6

129

Proportion and Distortion in Masks

Faustwork Mask Theater:
Robert Faust.

by wearing different masks, Robert Faust can make himself into many different characters. He surprises everyone with the funny faces and strange features of his masks. In many cultures throughout the world, masks are worn at festivals, celebrations, and rituals. Wherever they are used, masks make it possible for a person to pretend to be someone or something else.

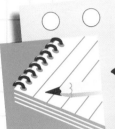

What To Do

Create a two-sided mask that shows contrasting feelings.

Materials

- ✓ paper plates, glue, and scissors
- ✓ paper towel tubes, yarn, buttons, fabric
- ✓ crayons and markers
- ✓ beans, rice, seeds, or other natural materials

1. Discuss pairs of emotions: happy/sad, mean/kind. Then, show an exaggeration of each of these feelings in your face.

2. Create two contrasting masks. Use a paper plate to sketch each face. Use distortion in the features. Decorate your masks. Then, fasten them back to back.

3. Make a slit in the end of the paper towel tube. Put the masks in the slit. Use the tube as a handle.

4. Develop movements that express the feelings on each mask. Perform your idea of two contrasting characters.

Describe Describe your two-sided mask.

Analyze Explain how you used distortion and exaggeration in creating your masks.

Interpret What opposite feelings did you create with your masks and your body?

Decide How well did you succeed in communicating two different emotions?

Extra Credit ·

Make a self-portrait mask. Present a pantomime of a particular event in your life.

Proportion
and Distortion
Reviewing Main Ideas

The lessons and activities in this unit show how proportion and distortion are used by artists to create both two- and three-dimensional works of art.

- **Proportion** is the principle of art concerned with the size relationships of one part to another.

- **Scale** is the principle of art referring to size as measured against a standard reference, like the human body. Scale can be created in two ways.

  1. **Realistic scale** is when an artist creates a work of art in which various elements seem to fit together well and they resemble size relations in real life.

  2. **Unrealistic scale** is when an artist intentionally makes size relationships that do not resemble real life.

- **Facial proportions** guidelines are used by an artist to correctly place features on the human face.

Edgar Degas. (French). *At the Milliner's.* 1882. Pastel on paper. 30 × 34 inches. The Metropolitan Museum of Art, New York, New York. Bequest of Mrs. H. O. Havemeyer, 1929. The H. O. Havemeyer Collection.

- **Exaggeration** is when an artist changes an object or person by enlarging a feature.
- **Distortion** is when an artist changes an object or person by changing a feature in any way except by enlarging it.

Summing Up

Look at the *At the Milliner's* by Edgar Degas. The artist used several of the proportion techniques taught in this unit.

- How does Degas use proportion in his painting?
- What type of scale does he use to relate the size of the two women in this painting?
- Has Degas exaggerated or distorted any of the features of the two women? Explain.

Proportion and distortion are used to create the illusion of realism or fantasy in a work of art. Artists use these principles to evoke the strong feelings they want to communicate.

Let's Visit a Museum

The Metropolitan Museum of Art in New York City is one of the world's largest museums. It has more than 2 million works of art spanning 5,000 years of culture. The museum was founded in 1870 and is located in the city's Central Park. Its Egyptian collection is second only to the one in Cairo, Egypt. Major collections in the museum in addition to the paintings include arms and armor, Chinese art, costumes, musical instruments, primitive art, French and American furniture, and photography. More than 4.5 million people from around the world visit the Metropolitan Museum each year.

The Metropolitan Museum of Art. 1991.

An Introduction to
Balance and Perspective

Some artists use balance and perspective to create a work of art.

Andrew Wyeth. (American). *Ground Hog Day.* 1959. Egg tempera on board. 31 × 31¾ inches. Philadelphia Museum of Art, Philadelphia, Pennsylvania. Given by Henry DuPont and Mrs. John Wintersteen.

Balance is used by artists to arrange visual elements in a work of art.

- When you look at this painting, what objects do you notice first?
- If you were to divide this painting in half, would both sides be identical?

Artists use **perspective** in paintings to create the illusion of depth.

- How does Wyeth create a feeling of depth in this painting?

Artist Profile

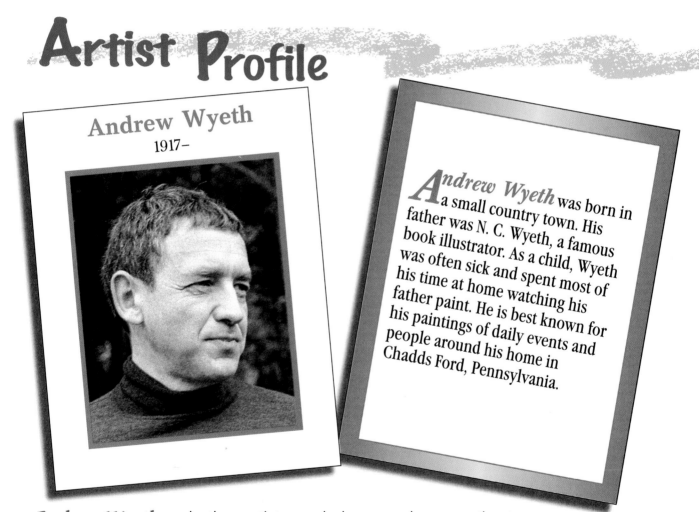

Andrew Wyeth
1917–

Andrew Wyeth was born in a small country town. His father was N. C. Wyeth, a famous book illustrator. As a child, Wyeth was often sick and spent most of his time at home watching his father paint. He is best known for his paintings of daily events and people around his home in Chadds Ford, Pennsylvania.

Andrew Wyeth and other artists use balance and perspective to arrange visual elements and create the illusion of depth. In this unit you will learn and practice the techniques that artists use to create balance and perspective in artworks. Here are the techniques.

- Types of Balance
- Depth
- Perspective
- Points of View

Formal Balance

Artists use formal balance to organize an artwork so that its opposite sides are equal or very similar.

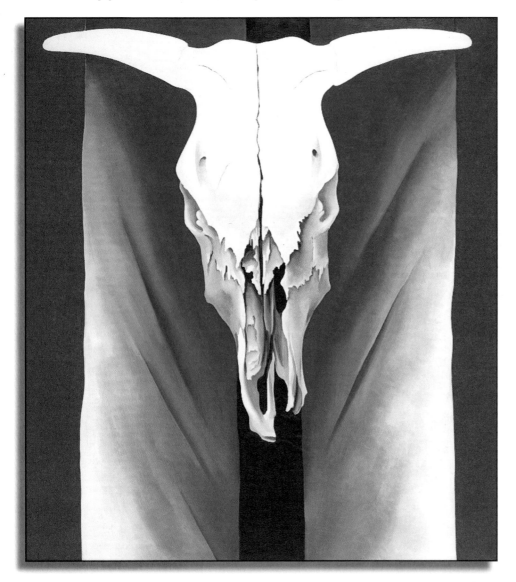

Georgia O'Keeffe. (American). *Cow's Skull: Red, White, and Blue*. 1931. Oil on canvas. $39\frac{7}{8} \times 35\frac{7}{8}$ inches. The Metropolitan Museum of Art, New York, New York. © The Georgia O'Keeffe Foundation/Artists Rights Society (ARS), New York.

Georgia O'Keeffe often painted images incorporating the New Mexico landscape and the remains of animals. Notice how the painting appears as if there were a line running down the middle of the cow's skull. In both paintings, the two sides are almost mirror images of each other. Chuck Close's *Self-Portrait* is an example of formal balance.

Chuck Close. (American). *Self Portrait.* 1987. Oil on canvas. 72 × 60 inches. Pace Wildenstein Gallery, New York, New York. Photo by Bill Jacobson.

Compare both paintings to find formal balance.

☑ Describe how the objects, colors, and lines are arranged in both works of art. How are they similar? How are they different?

☑ Find the center of each painting. What happens on either side of the center line?

☑ Are both sides of each painting identical? Where do you see differences?

Lesson 1

SEEING LIKE AN ARTIST

Can you think of any objects in nature that if divided in half would be identical on both sides?

Using Formal Balance

Balance is the principle of design that deals with visual weight in a work of art. One type of balance is **formal balance.**

Formal balance occurs when equal, or very similar, elements are placed on opposite sides of a central line called a **central axis**. The axis may be part of the design, or it may be an imaginary line. The axis, or central line, divides the design in half.

Symmetry is a special type of formal balance. The two halves of a symmetrically balanced object are the same. They are mirror images of each other.

Practice

Find examples of symmetrical balance in this book.

1. See if you can find individual objects in an artwork that you think are symmetrical.

2. Discuss why the work or objects are an example of symmetrical balance. Share with your class one example of symmetrical balance.

Decide Explain why you think your selection is a good example of symmetrical balance.

How do you know where the imaginary axis of the robot is?

Jason Starnes. Age 11. *Johnny the Racer.* Relief print.

Create

If you could design a personal robot, what would you have it do for you? Create a relief print of a robot using symmetrical balance.

1. Think about what tasks you want your robot to do. Draw your robot using symmetrical balance. Create a cardboard relief print. In a **relief print**, the image to be printed is raised from the background.

2. Draw on cardboard so that it has a central axis. Cut the shapes from the cardboard and glue them onto a printing plate (another piece of cardboard), keeping the symmetrical balance.

3. Use brayer and ink to make three prints of the robot.

Describe Describe the types of shapes you used to design your robot.

Analyze How did you use symmetry to arrange these shapes?

Interpret Does your robot look like what it is supposed to do? Give it a name.

Decide Do you think using symmetrical balance in this project was helpful?

Informal Balance

Informal balance occurs when two unlike **objects**
in an artwork have equal visual weight.

James Tissot. (French).
Women of Paris, The Circus Lover.
1883–85. Oil on canvas. 58 × 40
inches. Museum of Fine Arts,
Boston, Massachusetts. Juliana
Cheney Edwards Collection.

James Tissot was interested in portraying urban life at
the turn of the century. Notice how he arranged the
people in this painting. He has larger figures and darker colors
in the lower half, and smaller figures and brighter colors in
the upper half. In Sofonisba Anguissola's Italian Renaissance
painting, the placement of the figures is different. The figures
on the right are farther away from the center of the painting.
Notice how both artists use informal balance.

Sofonisba Anguissola. (Italian). *The Sisters of the Artist and their Governess/A game of chess, involving the painter's three sisters and a servant.* 1555. Oil on canvas. 72 × 97 cm. National Museum Poznan, Poland. Erich Lessing/Art Resource, New York.

Analyze both works of art to better understand informal balance.

☑ What are the important figures in each painting?

☑ How are the figures in these paintings arranged?

☑ Do objects take up one area or several areas in these two works?

☑ Where are the darkest and lightest areas in both paintings? How does this placement affect the mood of each?

SEEING LIKE AN ARTIST
Look for an area in your school where the items are arranged using informal balance.

Using Informal Balance

Informal balance is a way of organizing parts of a design so that unlike objects have equal visual weight. **Asymmetry** is another name for "informal balance." The **negative space**, or the areas around an object or group of objects, is often larger on one side of an asymmetrical piece than on the other side. There are several ways that artists create asymmetrical balance.

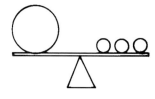

SIZE: A large shape or form will appear to be heavier than a small shape. Several small shapes can balance one large shape. To create informal balance, place large shapes closer to the center and small shapes farther away.

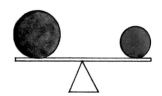

COLOR: A brighter color has more visual weight than a dull color.

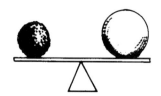

TEXTURE: A rough texture has an uneven pattern of highlights and shadows. For this reason, a rough surface attracts the viewer's eyes more easily than a smooth, even surface.

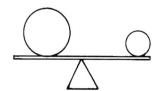

POSITION: A large, positive shape and a small, negative space can be balanced by a small, positive shape and a large, negative space.

Practice

Demonstrate informal or asymmetrical balance.

1. Form groups of four or five students. Choose one of the ways that artists use informal or asymmetrical balance.

2. Create a pose with your body to illustrate that particular type of balance. Have your classmates guess which type of balance technique your group is demonstrating.

Decide How did you communicate your technique? What pose did you use to help you communicate your technique?

Unit 5

Rachel Young. Age 11. *Potted Plant.* Watercolor.

How did the student artist create balance in the painting?

Create

What are the different types of objects around you that could be used for a still life? Create a still-life painting using asymmetrical balance.

1. Think about arranging an asymmetrically balanced still life. Collect the objects you have selected, then arrange them.

2. Use your thumb and index finger to form a frame around the still life to help you look at only one section of it. Lightly draw your selected section of the still life.

3. Add color and details to your drawing.

Describe What objects or section of the still life did you select to draw? What colors did you use?

Analyze Why did you select that particular area of the still life? How did you arrange the objects on your paper?

Interpret What feeling do you get when you look at your asymmetrical still life? Give it a title.

Decide Does your painting show asymmetrical balance? How?

Radial Balance

Artists use radial balance to enhance shapes and forms. Radial balance is found in natural objects and objects made by people.

Both works of art on these two pages once served as functional pieces. This means they were used and not just admired as works of art. The *Ardabil Carpet* was one of a pair of carpets that was donated as a gift to a royal shrine. It was used within the shrine, possibly as a prayer rug. The *Deep Dish* was once used as a serving bowl. The center section is a replica of a family coat of arms. The designs on both pieces are arranged very similarly. Notice how lines, shapes, and color are used and arranged.

Artist unknown. (Iran). *Ardabil Carpet.* 1540. Wool and silk. $23\frac{1}{2} \times 13$ feet. Los Angeles County Museum of Art, Los Angeles, California. Gift of J. Paul Getty.

Artist unknown. (Spain). *Deep Dish/Spain/from Valencia.* 1430. Tin-glazed earthenware painted in cobalt blue and lustre. 6.7 × 48.2 cm. Hispanic Society of America, New York, New York.

Study both works of art to see examples of radial design.

- ✓ Where is the center of each design?

- ✓ Find the shapes that start in the center and repeat as they move away from the center.

- ✓ Describe the designs you see. How are they arranged?

- ✓ Can you find where these designs begin and end?

SEEING LIKE AN ARTIST

What objects have you seen at school or at home that have designs that start in the center and repeat in a circular pattern?

Lesson 3

Using Radial Balance

Radial balance occurs when the elements of design (line, shape, color, and form) seem to radiate or come out from a center point. In almost every case, the elements are spaced evenly around the center of the design and create circular patterns.

Radial balance happens frequently in nature. Many plants follow radial patterns of growth. Cut an orange in half and you will see the radial pattern of the segments.

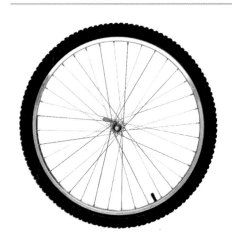

People have imitated nature in many objects by creating radial designs. You often see radial balance in architecture such as stained glass windows. The design always radiates out from a central point. Another example of radial balance is the bicycle wheel.

Practice

Create examples of radial designs using objects found in your classroom.

1. In small groups, collect objects from your desk or room.

2. Using your collected objects, arrange them into a design that has radial balance. Experiment with several arrangements.

Decide Look at all the designs in the class. Which design do you like best? Why?

What did the student artist use to create radial balance?

James D. Woods. Age 10. *My Future.* Yarn and magazine cutouts on posterboard.

Create

How would you create a balanced design to show your dreams for future? Create a collage design that has radial balance.

1. Think about your dreams of the future. Create a mandala of your dreams. A **mandala** is a radial design divided into sections or wedges, each of which contains a different image.

2. Cut out a round piece of posterboard for the background. Use yarn and found materials to divide the circle into wedges, creating the radial pattern. All wedges should be identical in size and have identical designs for a successful radial design.

3. Draw or cut out from magazines images that represent ideas you have for your future. Glue a different picture into each wedge.

Describe What objects did you use to press shapes into your design? What types of shapes did you use?

Analyze How did you organize your design?

Interpret What does your radial design remind you of? Why?

Decide Do you like the way you used your shapes and lines to create radial balance in your design? Can you think of other ways to create radial balance?

Perspective Techniques

Perspective techniques help artists make objects appear closer or farther away from the viewer.

Claude Monet. (French). *The Arrival of the Normandy Train at the Gare Saint-Lazare.* 1877. Oil on canvas. $23\frac{1}{2} \times 31\frac{1}{2}$ inches. Art Institute of Chicago, Mr. and Mrs. Martin Ryerson Collection, 1933. Chicago, Illinois.

Claude Monet is one of the greatest French Impressionist painters. Notice how he has portrayed the light and steam in this painting. Lismer grew as an artist when he painted the wild northern landscapes of Canada. He adopted the Impressionistic style for *The Guide's Home Algonquin,* using reflected light and broken brush strokes. Observe how both artists used lines, shapes, and colors.

Arthur Lismer. (Canadian). *The Guide's Home Algonquin.* 1914. Oil on canvas. 102.6 × 114.4 cm. National Gallery of Canada. Ottawa, Ontario, Canada.

Study both paintings to see how perspective techniques are used.

☑ Where is the middle ground of each painting? What objects are painted there?

☑ What objects are partially covering other objects?

☑ How do the colors, lines, and shapes change from the foreground to the background of each painting?

☑ Do you see a set of lines in Monet's work where the lines look like they are getting closer together?

SEEING LIKE AN ARTIST

Look across your classroom. How do the objects look that are far away from you? How do those objects look when you get closer to them?

Lesson 4

Using Perspective Techniques

Perspective is the method used to create the illusion of depth on a flat surface, like a drawing or painting. **Depth** is the appearance of distance on a flat surface. There are six different perspective techniques that artists can use to create the feeling of depth.

 OVERLAPPING: When one object partially covers another object, the object in front appears to be closer.

 **SIZE:** Large objects seem to be closer to the viewer than small objects. The smaller the object, the farther away it appears to be, unless it is placed on top of something large in the front of the picture.

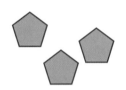 **LOCATION:** Objects placed near the bottom of a picture seem to be closer to the viewer. Objects placed near the top of a picture seem to be farther away.

 **DETAIL:** Objects with clear, sharp edges and details appear to be closer to the viewer. Objects with fuzzy edges and without details seem to be farther away.

 **LINES:** Parallel lines seem to move toward the same point as they move farther away from the viewer.

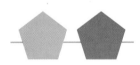 **COLOR:** Brightly colored objects seem closer to the viewer. Objects with pale, dull colors seem to be farther away.

Practice

Discover perspective techniques.

1. Look around the classroom. List examples of each perspective technique that you observe.

2. Describe the techniques that you see.

Decide Why do some objects look closer? Why do some objects look larger than others?

Sara Flowers. Age 10. *Scarecrow from the Wizard of Oz*. Watercolor.

What techniques did the student artist use to create an illusion of depth in the picture?

Create

What are some scenes that come to mind when you hear your favorite song? Design a fantasy setting for a music video using perspective techniques.

1. Think about your favorite song. Make a sketch of a fantasy scene that could be used as the background for a music video.

2. Think about the perspective techniques that create depth. Use at least four of the six perspective techniques in your scene.

3. Add color to your fantasy scene, and title your work. Write the name of the song you were thinking of on the back of your paper.

Describe Describe the lines, shapes, colors, and objects in your fantasy scene.

Analyze Which perspective technique did you use to create depth?

Interpret What mood did you create in your fantasy scene? Does the scene suggest the mood of your song?

Decide Were you successful in creating illusion of depth? What techniques were most effective? Explain.

Lesson 4

151

Linear Perspective

Artists use linear perspective to create the
illusion of depth in a piece of artwork.

Giovanni Paolo Pannini. (Italian). *Interior of St. Peters, Rome.* 1754. Oil on canvas.
$60\frac{3}{4} \times 77\frac{1}{2}$ inches. National Gallery, Washington, DC. Ailsa Mellon Bruce Fund.
© 1996 Board of Trustees, National Gallery of Art, Washington, DC.

*I*nterior *of St. Peters, Rome,* was painted by Pannini.
He was the first artist to specialize in painting
architectural ruins. Edward Hicks used flat forms with clearly
defined edges. He was considered a primitive artist. This
means he had no formal training. He painted scenes from the
Bible, the farm, and historical America. Both artists use similar
techniques to make the viewer look into the distance.

Edward Hicks. (American). *Cornell Farm*. 1848. Oil on canvas. $36\frac{3}{4} \times 49$ inches. National Gallery of Art, Washington, DC. Gift of Edgar William and Bernice Chrysler Garbisch, © 1996 Board of Trustees, National Gallery of Art, Washington DC.

Analyze both paintings to discover linear perspective.

✓ Follow the lines of the walls and fields that lead to the area that looks farthest away from the viewer.

✓ What types of shapes are repeated in each painting? What happens to these shapes the farther away they become?

✓ Find objects in both paintings that overlap.

✓ Where are the largest and smallest objects?

✓ Describe the use of details in both works of art.

SEEING LIKE AN ARTIST

What does a road look like as you move away from it in a car? Does the road really get smaller?

Using Linear Perspective

Perspective is the method used to create the illusion of depth on a flat surface. Often when artists want to make viewers think they are looking at an object moving back into space, they use one-point linear perspective.

Linear perspective is one way of using lines to show distance and depth. All lines that move back into space meet at a single point in one-point perspective.

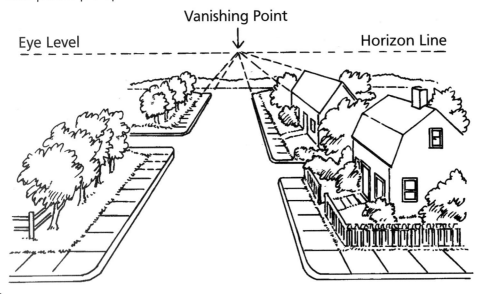

The **horizon line** is the point at which the earth and sky meet. In the example above, the horizon line is at eye level.

The **vanishing point** is the point on the horizon line where all the lines moving back into space meet. Can you find the vanishing point in Pannini's painting?

Practice

Practice seeing linear perspective.

1. Look down the end of a hallway to the farthest possible point. Close one eye and raise your index fingers to the lines where the wall and ceiling meet. Move your fingers along those lines until they reach the end of the hall. Notice how your arms move down to eye level.

2. Do this again, pointing to the lines where the walls meet the floor. How did your arms move?

Describe What did you observe when doing this sighting technique? Where did your hands meet? Do you see how linear perspective is created?

Unit 5

Sally Brannen. Age 11. *Small Town Street.* Watercolor.

Which objects have lines that lead to the vanishing point?
Where is the vanishing point?

Create

How can you use linear perspective in a real or imaginary scene? Draw a real or imaginary scene that has the illusion of depth. Include at least one building that uses linear perspective.

1. Think of a real or imaginary place. Make several sketches of objects you want to include in your scene. Include at least one building.

2. Lightly draw a horizon line and mark a point on it where the lines will meet. Draw at least four lines coming out from the point on the horizon line. This is the vanishing point. Using these guidelines, draw the building first, then the other objects. Make the objects touch the top and bottom of the guidelines.

3. Paint your drawing.

Describe Did you draw a real or imaginary scene? What objects did you include in your scene?

Analyze How did you use linear perspective in your work?

Interpret What objects communicate the kind of scene you created? Give your work a title.

Decide How could you apply the technique of linear perspective to another drawing?

Point of View and Direct Observation

Artists will often study an object from different points of view before creating an artwork.

Edward Hopper. (American). *House by the Railroad.* 1925. Oil on canvas.
24 × 29 inches. The Museum of Modern Art, New York, New York.
Given anonymously. © 1998.

Notice how both artists created images from different angles. *House by the Railroad* was painted during a time of migration from farms to the cities. Charles Sheeler is best known for his simplified paintings of industrial landscapes. He uses simple shapes and flat colors. Can you tell where each artist is standing in relation to his work?

Charles Sheeler. (American). *American Interior.* 1934. Oil on canvas. $32\frac{1}{2}$ x 30 inches. Yale Art Gallery. Gift of Mrs. Paul Moore.

Study both paintings for their use of viewpoint.

✓ Where are you in relation to the paintings? Are you looking up at the paintings, down onto the paintings, or directly at the paintings?

✓ Do the shapes and lines look like they are drawn from a particular angle? How does this affect the use of shadows?

✓ Why do you think each artist chose to create his painting from these angles?

SEEING LIKE AN ARTIST

Hold up this book and look at it from different angles. What happens to the shape, shadows, and lines?

Using Point of View and Direct Observation

Point of view is the angle from which you see an object or scene. Depending on the point of view, the way you perceive, or see, an object can change. There are four common points of view. Notice how your perception changes as you look at the same object from various points of view.

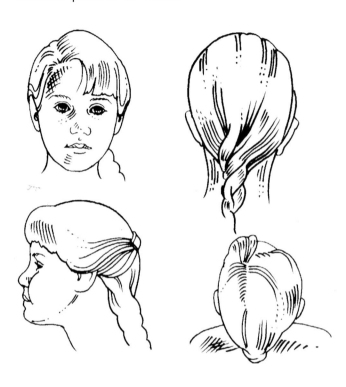

Often artists study an object from various viewpoints. They look closely at the important details and record them in their drawings. This approach is called **direct observation**

Practice

Select one object and describe it from one viewpoint.

1. Working in small groups, take turns selecting one object from the classroom and describing what it looks like from your viewpoint.

2. Use the elements of art, shape, line, and texture to help you describe your object. Let the group guess what your object is.

Decide Could your friends tell what you were describing? Were they able to guess which angle you were viewing the object from?

Ashley Davis. Age 9. *Strawberry.*
Crayon and watercolor.

What three views of the strawberry did the student artist show? How can you tell?

Create

How does shape change as you change your point of view? Create one drawing of an object from three different points of view.

1. Think about how an object looks from different points of view. Notice how the shadows and shapes of an object change when you are looking at it from different points of view.

2. Draw an object from three points of view.

Describe Describe the object that you observed and the details you noticed.

Analyze What three points of view did you select? Why?

Interpret Give your work a title.

Decide How does drawing an object from more than one point of view change your understanding of the object?

Balance and Perspective in Dance

"Los Concheros": *Ballet Folklorico de Mexico.*

In ancient cultures, people performed folk dances that connected them to life and the universe. They used dance movements as symbols of things in nature such as the moon and the sun. In their folk dances, they achieved balance through repetition of lines and forms. They showed depth through their movements.

What To Do

Create dance designs that are symbols of the sun.

Materials

✓ a variety of symbols and designs based on the image of the sun

1. Look at the different symbols or designs of the sun. In each work, notice the use of balance and perspective.

2. Brainstorm elements of these works that could be shown in a dance design.

3. With a group, explore ways that you can use the shapes and lines of your bodies to create symbols of the sun.

4. Select three of your best designs, and put them in an interesting sequence.

5. Perform your designs for other groups.

Describe Describe the main design elements that you used in creating your sun dance.

Analyze Explain how you used balance and depth in your dance.

Interpret How did your dance portray the sun expressively?

Decide How well did you succeed in capturing the image of the sun? What would you change if you did this again?

Extra Credit · · · · · · · · · · · · · · · · ·

Add sounds to your dance with percussion instruments, such as a gong, drum, woodblock, finger cymbals, and shakers.

Balance and Perspective

Reviewing Main Ideas

The lessons and activities in this unit cover the techniques that artists use to create balance and perspective.

- **Balance** — A principle of design that deals with arranging visual elements equally in a work of art. There are two types of balance.

  1. **Formal or symmetrical balance** occurs when equal, or very similar, elements are placed on opposite sides of a central line called an axis.

  2. **Radial balance** occurs when the elements of design seem to radiate or come out of a center point.

3. **Informal or asymmetrical balance** is a balance of unlike objects. It is a way of organizing part of a design so that unlike objects have equal visual weight. It is not exactly the same on both sides.

- **Depth** is the appearance of distance on a flat surface.

- **Perspective** is the method used to create the illusion of depth on a flat surface.

Gustave Caillebotte. (French). *Paris Street Rainy Day.* 1876–1877. Oil on canvas. 212.2 × 276.2 cm. Art Institute of Chicago, Chicago, Illinois. Charles H. and Mary F. S. Worcester Collection.

There are six perspective techniques: overlapping, size, location, detail, lines, and color.

- **One-point perspective** is when lines move back into space and meet at a single point to show distance and depth on a two-dimensional surface.
- **Horizon line** is the point at which the earth and sky meet.
- **Vanishing point** is the point on the horizon line where all the lines moving back into space meet.
- **Point of view** is the angle from which you see an object or scene. There are four common points of view: front, side, back, and overhead.

Summing Up

Look at *Paris Street, Rainy Day* by Gustave Caillebotte. In this painting, he used the techniques of creating balance and perspective covered in this unit.

- Explain the type of balance the artist used in the painting.
- Did Caillebotte use all six perspective techniques? Give examples of each perspective technique he used.

Balance and perspective are important elements in paintings and drawings. With balance and perspective, Caillebotte and other artists are able to arrange visual elements so that they are pleasing to the eye and create the illusion of depth.

Let's Visit a Museum

The Art Institute of Chicago was originally called the Chicago Academy of Fine Arts when it was established in 1879. Today, its membership is 150,000, the highest of any art museum in the country. Its collection has more than 225,000 works of art. There are ten different departments and galleries. The museum is known for its architectural displays and collection of French Impressionist works. A large part of the museum is a school. People from all over the world attend classes in photography, painting, fashion design, and other visual arts.

The Art Institute of Chicago

An Introduction to
Emphasis, Variety, Harmony, and Unity

Artists sometimes use emphasis, variety, harmony, and unity in paintings and sculptural forms.

John Biggers. (American). *Shotguns Fourth Ward.* 1987.
Acrylic and oil on board. $41\frac{3}{4} \times 32$ inches. Hampton
University Museum, Hampton, Virginia.

Emphasis is used by artists to attract attention to a certain area in a piece of artwork.

- What area of this painting do you see first?

Variety is used to make a drawing or painting more interesting.

- What shapes, lines, and colors are used more than once in this painting?

Artists sometimes use variety and **harmony** to create unity in a work of art.

- What element of this painting gives you a feeling of oneness and wholeness?

Artist Profile

John Biggers
1924–

John Biggers was born in Gastonia, North Carolina. He gives his parents the credit for encouraging his interest in human nature and for his ability to see beauty in almost anything. He first entered college to study heating and engineering, but a teacher inspired him to change his major to art. In addition to his work as an artist, he has also made important contributions as an art educator. His artworks include painting, sculpture, and murals.

John Biggers and other artists use emphasis, variety, harmony, and unity to attract attention to certain art elements, make a work of art more interesting, and create oneness or wholeness within a work of art. In this unit you will learn and practice the techniques that artists use. Here are the topics you will study.

- Emphasis
- Focal Point
- Variety
- Unity
- Harmony

Emphasis Through Contrast

Artists use color, shape, and size to emphasize
or draw attention to an area in an artwork.

Anne Beard. (American). *Rodeo Jacket.* Courtesy of Ms. Anne Beard. U.S. Seminole.

Anne Beard created *Rodeo Jacket* using a technique
called appliqué. **Appliqué** is made by attaching fabric
shapes onto a fabric background by gluing or sewing. *Ponca
Blouse* was created out of cloth and ribbon work. Traditionally,
Ponca artists added an odd bead to their costumes or broke
the pattern in some other way so that the costumes weren't
perfect. They felt this was a way to be humble. Both works of
art are examples of emphasis through contrast.

Artist unknown. *Blouse.* Ponca Tribe. Woman's cloth waist shirt decorated with ribbon work. Smithsonian National Museum of the American Indian, New York, New York.

Compare both works of art to better understand emphasis through contrast.

✓ Describe how the objects, colors, and lines are arranged in both works of art.

✓ Close your eyes, then open them, looking at one of the images. What was the first thing that you saw? Why do you think this happened?

✓ Which one of the two pieces tells a story?

✓ Which of these two works of art would you like to wear?

SEEING LIKE AN ARTIST

Think about an advertisement you may have seen that you really liked. What objects or colors drew your attention? Why?

Using Emphasis

Emphasis is the principle of design that stresses one area in a work of art. Have you ever underlined or highlighted an important word in your study notes? Have you ever seen an advertisement or video in which one object seemed to jump out and catch your attention? These are examples of emphasis.

There are several techniques that artists use to create emphasis.

Contrast occurs when one element stands out from the rest of the work. A bright color will stand out from a dull color. A large shape will stand out from small shapes. An angular shape among round shapes will catch your attention.

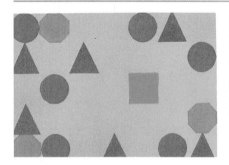

Isolation happens when an object is placed alone and away from all the other objects in an artwork. The viewer's eye then looks at the isolated object.

Location occurs when the eyes are naturally drawn toward the center of an artwork. Anything placed near the center of the picture will be noticed first.

Practice

Find examples of emphasis through contrast. Use newspapers and magazines.

1. What word or object in each attracts your eye first? Is it because of size, color, or an unusual shape? Locate three examples of emphasis through contrast.

2. Highlight the word or object emphasized in each example.

Decide What about the word or object in each example caught your attention first?

What kind of emphasis did the student artist use?

Tia Clyburn. Age 11.
Untitled. Appliqué stitchery.

Create

What symbol best represents your interests or tells something about you? Use appliqué to create a design showing emphasis through contrast on an article of clothing or a piece of material.

1. Think about a symbol to draw and cut out from fabric that represents something about you. Your symbol will become your appliqué and the point of emphasis.

2. Use emphasis techniques to draw several sketches of your symbol. Select one sketch for your symbol.

3. Trace the symbol onto the fabric and cut it out. Stitch the symbol onto your selected fabric. Decorate your appliqué with different types of stitches.

Describe Describe the symbol that you selected and the types of stitches that you used to complete your appliqué.

Analyze How does the symbol create a point of emphasis on the background?

Interpret Does your appliqué clearly communicate something about you and your interests?

Decide Did strong contrast make the clothing or fabric look better? Why?

Emphasis as a Focal Point

Emphasis is used by artists to draw attention to a specific area in a work of art.

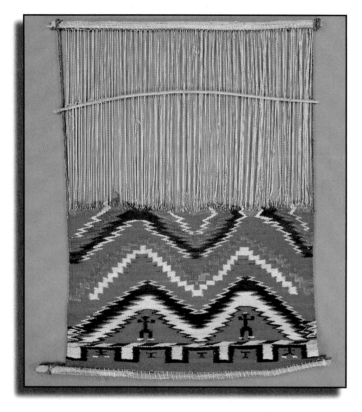

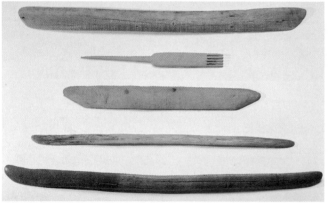

Artist unknown. Top: Navajo loom with wool blanket. Bottom: Battens, comb, and spreading stick. 113.1 × 104.2 cm. Loom with partly woven blanket. New York, New York. Smithsonian Institution National Museum of the American Indian, William M. Fitzhugh Collection.

Although *Navajo Loom* is a half-completed, woven blanket, you can see that the emphasized area, or the focal point, is the two small figures. Both weavings have a distinct design that represents the individual woman who wove it, her people, and a story. In *Crow, Crow,* the focal point is the crow. Both artists used symbols and designs to create their weaving patterns. The first thing that attracts the viewer's attention in each work is the focal point.

Tommye Scanlin. (American). *Crow, Crow.* 6 × 6 inches. Wool, cotton. Courtesy of Tommye Scanlin.

Analyze both works of art to better understand emphasis as a focal point.

✓ What do you think are the most important objects or areas in both these works of art? Why?

✓ How are the lines, shapes, and colors in these works of art arranged?

✓ What area of each piece attracts your eye? Why?

SEEING LIKE AN ARTIST
Close your eyes, then open them. What is the first thing you see? What about it drew your attention?

Using Emphasis as a Focal Point

Emphasis is usually the most important area of an artwork. It helps unify a work of art. Emphasis controls the order in which the viewer notices the parts and the amount of attention the viewer gives each part. The area emphasized is called the **focal point**. Artists use different techniques to create a focal point:

 Using a contrasting color on one object or shape creates a focal point. The orange circle is the focal point.

 Using a contrasting shape or form will create a focal point. The solid rectangle is the focal point.

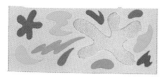 Using a contrasting size will create a focal point. The focal point is the large shape.

 Location near the center of a work creates a focal point. Placing one object near the center of a composition will make that object the focal point of the work.

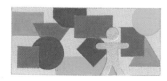 Difference will create a focal point. The human form is the focal point.

Practice

Talk about the focal point of your school.

1. Form groups. Discuss within the groups the emphasis or focal point of your school.

2. What physical characteristics make up its focal point? Compare opinions and share with the class.

Decide How did you decide what made up the focal point of the school? Did everyone in your group agree?

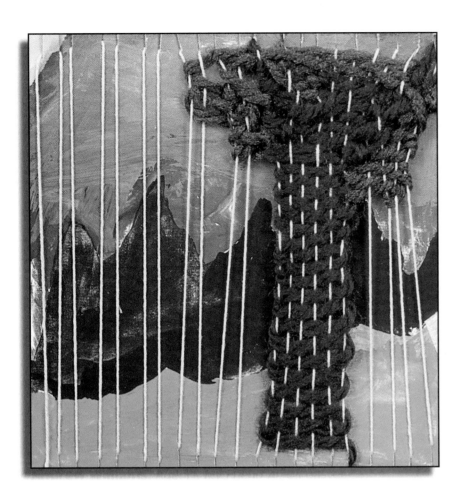

What is the focal point of this artwork?

Jennifer Keeler. Age 10. *My Tree.* Fibers, tempera paint on posterboard.

Create

What part of a landscape scene do you find most interesting? Create a focal point in a mixed-media work of art.

1. Think about part of a landscape you like. Draw several sketches.

2. Make a cardboard loom and draw one sketch onto it. Fill your drawing with color. String the warp threads over the drawing. **Warp** threads are the vertical threads attached to the loom.

3. Outline with yarn onto the warp threads the shape that will be the focal point of your work. Hold the outline in place with pieces of tape. Fill the shape with weft threads. **Weft** threads are threads that are woven over and under the warp threads.

Describe What type of landscape did you create? What object did you select to weave onto your loom?

Analyze Why did you select that particular area of the landscape to weave your object?

Interpret Give your work a title.

Decide Do you think that other people will recognize where the focal point of your work is? What will cause them to look there first?

Variety

Artists use variety to add interest to their artwork.

Janet Fish. (American). *After Leslie Left.* 1983–84. Oil on canvas. 48 × 62 inches.
Albright Knox Art Gallery, Buffalo, New York. Norman E. Boasberg, George Cary,
and Charles W. Goodyear Funds, 1984.

Janet Fish is best known for her realistic paintings of objects. She is interested in showing how light plays on surfaces such as mirrors, glass, and metals. Romare Bearden is best known for his collages made from pieces of old photographs, scraps of paper, and painted papers. Both artworks use variety.

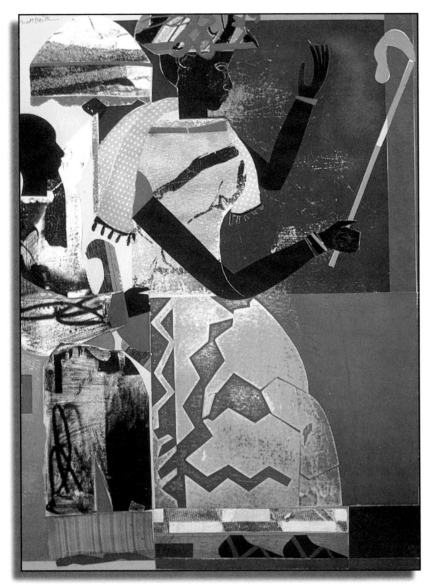

Romare Bearden. (American). *She Ba.* 1970. Paper, cloth, paint, board. $48 \times 35\frac{7}{8}$ inches. Wadsworth Atheneum, Hartford, Connecticut. The Ella Gallup Sumner and Mary Catlin Sumner Collection Fund. © Romare Bearden Foundation/Licensed by VAGA, New York, NY.

Compare both works of art to learn about variety.

✓ Compare the types of lines, colors, and shapes used by both artists.

✓ What did both artists do to add interest to their works of art?

✓ Describe the different objects you see in each picture. How are they arranged?

SEEING LIKE AN ARTIST

What is your favorite display in a shop window or at the mall? Are the colors, patterns, and objects the same or different?

Using Variety

Variety is the principle of design concerned with difference or contrast. If a work has no variety—for instance, it is a painting of one shape in one color—it probably will not hold the viewer's attention. When different elements, like lines, shapes, or colors, are placed next to each other in a work of art, they are in **contrast**. This adds interest to the artwork and gives it a lively quality.

Lines, shapes, and colors are three of the elements of art that are used to create variety in a work of art.

Variety in Lines

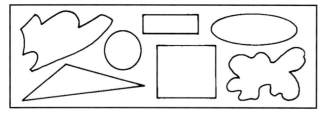

Variety in Shapes

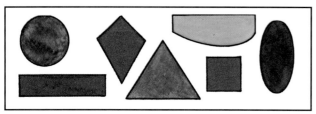

Variety in Colors

Practice

Use variety to redesign a common household item. Use markers.

1. Think of a common household object, such as a tube of toothpaste, a box of laundry detergent, a bar of soap, or a spoon.

2. Use colored markers to draw the object. Add variety or contrast to your selected object by using contrasting lines, shapes, or colors.

Decide Do you think your new design is more interesting than the original design? Did you create variety or contrast?

How did the student artist use variety to make the work more interesting?

Brent Lennox. Age 11. *Colorful Building*. Marker.

Create

What area of your school could be improved? Use variety to change an area of your school to make it more interesting.

1. Think about an area in or around your school that you think is dull or uninteresting. What are some changes you can make without losing the area's purpose?

2. Create two sketches of the area. Experiment with some ways to add variety or contrast using either color, lines, or shapes.

3. Reproduce one onto your paper. Add color. The area needs to remain functional but should be more interesting than before.

Describe What changes did you make to your selected area?

Analyze How did you organize your design?

Interpret What one word best describes your design?

Decide Do you like the changes you made? Can you think of other ways to create variety or contrast in this area of your school?

Harmony

Artists use harmony in their artwork to create a feeling of unity.

John Biggers has painted about twenty murals using the topic of the black experience in America and Africa. The people in Biggers's work are unique and dignified. Diego Rivera was a muralist who was invited to paint many murals in the United States in the 1930s. He emphasized the dignity of working people.

John Biggers. (American). *Tree House.* 1990–92. Acrylic on canvas. 240 × 120 inches. Hampton University Museum, Hampton, VA. William R. and Norma B. Harvey Library.

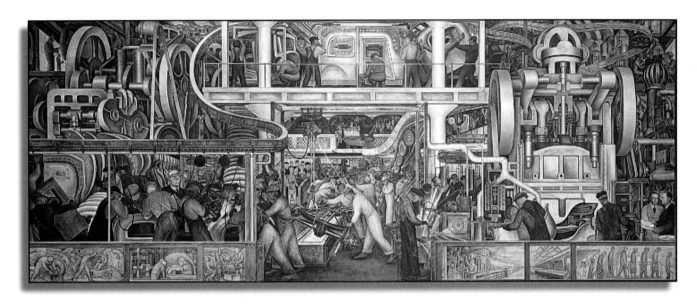

Diego Rivera. (Mexican). *Detroit Industry (Mural)—South Wall*. 1932–33. Fresco. 43 × 67 feet.
The Detroit Institute of Arts, Detroit, Michigan. Photograph © 1996. Gift of Edsel B. Ford.

Observe how harmony is used in both paintings.

- ✓ Do you see any lines, shapes, or colors repeated in either mural?

- ✓ Is there any one area in either mural that seems to stand out? If so, what area is it?

- ✓ How would you describe the use of color in both works?

- ✓ Do you think these artists took a long time to plan these murals? Why or why not?

SEEING LIKE AN ARTIST

Think about a costume or a uniform. What made the costume or uniform look like the pieces were meant to be worn together? Was it a particular color, texture, or pattern?

Using Harmony

Harmony is the principle of design that is concerned with similarities of separate but related parts. Artists use these art elements to create harmony.

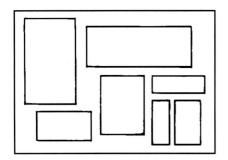

Shapes create harmony when related shapes of various sizes are repeated. A design using one type of shape is more harmonious than a design using two types of shapes.

Color creates harmony when a work is limited to only cool or warm colors.

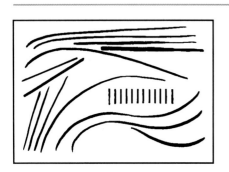

Line creates harmony by limiting lines to either straight or curved lines.

Practice

Arrange a still life to observe harmony. Use items of the same color.

1. As a class, choose one color. Have each person in the class bring in an item of the selected color.

2. Form small groups and create a still life using the objects brought to class. Discuss in small groups how color creates harmony in the still life.

Decide What types of objects were displayed in your group's still life? How did the use of color create harmony?

Tiffany Hayes. Age 9. *The Encounter.* Wood scraps, tempera.

How does the student artist create harmony in
the assemblage?

Create

**How can you arrange unrelated objects in an
artwork to create harmony? Design an
assemblage using color to create harmony.**

1. Think about harmony and how one element,
such as color, can pull a variety of objects
together.

2. Collect all found materials. These items will be
used to create an assemblage. An **assemblage**
is a sculpture in which a variety of objects are
assembled to create one complete piece.

3. Arrange a few items at a time. Glue them into
place. Let your assemblage dry, then paint it
using related colors.

Describe Describe the objects
you used in your assemblage. Are
textures similar or different? Are
the objects of various sizes?

Analyze Was there any particular
order to the arrangement of your
objects?

Interpret Were you able to create
the feeling of harmony within
your assemblage? What
differences do you notice when
you look at your piece by itself
and when you add it to a group?

Decide What color did you
choose as a class? Did this color
bring together the completed
work?

Environmental Unity

Artists often use harmony and variety to
create unity in a work of art.

William M. Chase. (American). *The Park*. 1888. Oil on canvas. $13\frac{5}{8} \times 19\frac{5}{8}$ inches.
Art Institute of Chicago, Chicago, Illinois. Bequest of Dr. John J. Ireland.

William Merritt Chase was a very successful
artist best known for his portraits, landscapes, and
still lifes. Chase became interested in the effects of light.
Playground equipment sometimes looks like sculpture when
the playground is designed by an artist. This piece of
equipment is a slide. The forms around the slide have been
designed to look like a futuristic creature. Both artists use
harmony and variety to create unity in their artwork.

Artist unknown. (Jerusalem). *Playground.* National Geographic Image Collection.

Study both works of art to find harmony and variety in each.

✓ What colors stand out most in both works of art?

✓ What types of shapes and lines do you see repeated in each artwork?

✓ Is there any one element that you notice more than others?

✓ What are some differences you notice between the two? Do these differences create a particular mood?

SEEING LIKE AN ARTIST

Think about how all the separate parts of your home, though they are different, work together to create a whole.

Using Unity

Unity is the feeling of wholeness or oneness that is achieved by properly using the elements and principles of art.

Unity is oneness. A plant is an example of unity in nature. It is made of a root system, a stem and leaves, and flowers. Each part has a purpose or job that gives life to the growing plant. Unity is created when harmony and variety work together.

Harmony and variety are two principles of art that work together to create unity. **Harmony** is the principle of art concerned with similarity or how separate parts relate. **Variety** is the opposite of harmony. It is about difference or contrast. A good balance between harmony and variety creates unity.

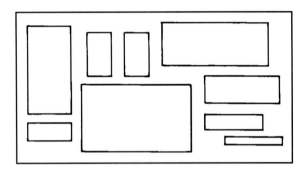

Harmony of Shapes

Variety of Shapes

Practice

Discover harmony and variety in your neighborhood.

1. Discuss in small groups what elements or objects create variety in your neighborhood. Discuss how the elements relate to create harmony.

2. Describe how variety and harmony work together.

Decide What elements did you describe? How is unity created through variety and harmony?

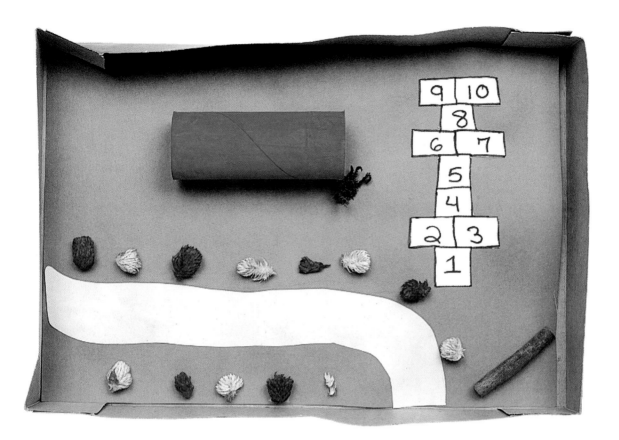

Ophelia Darst. Age 10. *Playground*. Found objects.

How does the student artist create unity for the piece of equipment she designed?

Create

What was your favorite playground when you were younger? Design one piece of equipment for a playground.

1. Think about a playground you remember. Choose one piece of equipment to create and make a sketch of it.

2. What does each separate part look like and how are the parts attached? Use paper and sculpture techniques to create your playground equipment.

3. Create the ground. Paint or glue down pathways, a hopscotch outline, or some flowers. Arrange your completed form on your prepared playground area.

Describe What piece of equipment did you select and how did you form it? What color is your playground equipment?

Analyze How did you arrange the various pieces? Describe how you used variety to create your equipment.

Interpret What title would you give the finished piece?

Decide What part of the scene do you like most? Do you feel that you were able to create unity by balancing harmony and variety?

Lesson 5

185

Unity

Artists create unity by bringing different objects or elements together in a work of art so that everything fits together.

Iris Sandkühler. *Composition in Brown and Gold.* 1995. Costume jewelry, copper, brass, glass, and amber. 24-inch length × 3-inch fringe. Private Collection.

The artist, Iris Sandkühler, uses many unusual materials to create jewelry. In *Composition in Brown and Gold,* she uses recycled jewelry. In the pendant, *Pyrite Sun Pendant,* she uses a unique process called *copper electroforming.* This process actually allows a designer to "grow" copper by combining chemical and electrical techniques. Notice how both pieces contain a variety of art elements yet create the feeling of wholeness.

Iris Sandkühler. (American). *Pyrite Sun Pendant.* 1992.
7 × 4 inches. Copper, brass, pyrite, sterling, glass, base
metal. Photograph: Sandkühler. Private Collection.

Compare the use of unity in both pieces of jewelry.

✓ What particular shapes do you recognize in each piece
of jewelry?

✓ Are there any unusual objects in either piece? How do
they relate to the work as a whole?

✓ What are some similarities and differences in each
piece?

SEEING LIKE
AN ARTIST
How do all the
different parts of a car
work together to
create a whole? What
would happen if one
part were missing?

Lesson 6

Using Unity

Unity is the quality of wholeness or oneness that is achieved through the effective use of the elements and principles of art.

Unity is oneness. It brings order to the world. It helps you concentrate on a visual image. When an artwork does not have unity, it is very difficult to concentrate on the work as a whole because all the different parts demand separate attention. It is like trying to talk to your friend when someone is playing a loud radio and a dog is barking. To create unity, an artist adjusts all parts of a work so that they relate to each other.

Practice

Observe an example of unity.

1. Find one example of unity in a piece of art in this book. Write the title, the artist, and the location of the artwork.

2. Discuss in a small group why you chose this work of art and how you think unity was created in it.

Decide What art elements are used to create unity in the work of art? What is it about this piece that first drew your attention?

How do the student artists maintain a sense of unity in the necklace?
Alia Whitney and **Claire Stanhope**.
Ages 10. *Necklace.* Mixed found objects.

Create

How is unity maintained when making a piece of jewelry with many objects? Create an original piece of jewelry, such as a badge or necklace, using found objects.

1. Think about the things around you that might look good as a piece of jewelry.

2. Arrange the materials to create your badge or necklace. Notice the changes that occur when you rearrange the materials.

3. Select one arrangement. Attach the materials to create one complete and unified piece. Glue a backing onto your badge or add a chain or piece of yarn to complete your necklace.

Describe Describe the materials used to create your jewelry. What colors and shapes are in your piece?

Analyze How did you arrange your materials to create unity? What other art elements created unity in your finished piece?

Interpret Does your ornament remind you of anything you have seen before? If so, what is it?

Decide What part of your completed piece do you like best? Why? Do you feel that you were able to create a feeling of unity in your work?

Emphasis, Variety, Harmony, and Unity in Music

Paul Tracey, songwriter.

Paul Tracey is a person who has used his experiences, whether they were sad, happy, frustrating, or funny, as a source for creative ideas. For example, when he got married and had a daughter, his new feelings of love and family closeness inspired him to write songs. His songs express the harmony of music, the variety of his experiences, and the wholeness, or unity, of his life.

▲ R T
S ● U
R C ◼
ARTSOURCE
•

What To Do

Write a song.

Materials

✔ paper and pencils

1. Choose the method you will use to write a song. You can write both the words and the music. You can put the words of a poem to original music. You can borrow a melody and write your own words.

2. Select a theme or idea for your song. Next, create a word web to identify words that relate to your theme. Then, find words that rhyme with those words.

3. Write words on your theme in rhythmic lines that end with rhyming words.

4. Try singing your song. Change the parts that don't seem to work. Practice and then perform it.

Describe Describe the songwriting method you used.

Analyze Explain how you used emphasis, harmony, variety, and unity in your song.

Interpret What feelings or mood does your song express?

Decide How well do you think you succeeded in writing a song? What would you do differently if you tried again?

Extra Credit

Accompany your song with a musical instrument or with sounds you have tape-recorded from nature. Perform for your class.

Emphasis, Variety, Harmony, and Unity

Reviewing Main Ideas

The lessons and activities in this unit cover the techniques that artists use to create emphasis, variety, harmony, and unity.

- **Emphasis** is the principle of design that stresses one area in a work of art.

- **Focal point** is the first thing in an artwork that attracts the attention of a viewer.

- **Variety** is the principle of design concerned with difference or contrast.

- **Unity** is the feeling of wholeness or oneness.

- **Harmony** is concerned with the similarities of separate but related parts. Similar art elements, such as line and shape, are combined to create visual harmony.

Edward Hopper. (American). *Railroad Sunset*. 1929. Oil on canvas. $28\frac{1}{4} \times 47\frac{3}{4}$ inches. Collection of Whitney Museum of American Art, New York/Josephine N. Hopper bequest/Photography by Bill Jacobson, N.Y.

Summing Up

Look at *Railroad Sunset* by Edward Hopper. In this painting, the artist created emphasis, variety, harmony, and unity covered in this unit.

- What is the first thing you see when you look at the painting *Railroad Sunset*?
- How did Edward Hopper use variety in this painting?
- How did Hopper create harmony and unity in his painting?

Emphasis, variety, harmony, and unity are all important art elements in works of art. By creating emphasis, variety, harmony, and unity, artists express what they see and feel to others.

Careers in Art
Jewelry Designer

Iris Sandkühler is a jewelry designer who was born in West Germany. Jewelry designers must have a good understanding of the elements of design. They must also understand the chemicals that make up different metals. The majority of Sandkühler's jewelry is made from a special process using copper. This is a process that uses chemicals and electricity to grow copper on glass. Sandkühler was asked to design an ornament for the White House Christmas tree using this special process. She says that although designing jewelry takes a lot of patience, she loves the challenge of coming up with new ideas.

Iris Sandkühler, jewelry designer

Technique Tips

Pencil

With the side of your pencil lead, press harder and shade over areas more than once for darker values. With a pencil, you can add form to your objects by shading. You can also use lines or dots for shading. When lines or dots are drawn close together, you get darker values. When dots or lines are drawn farther apart, lighter values are created.

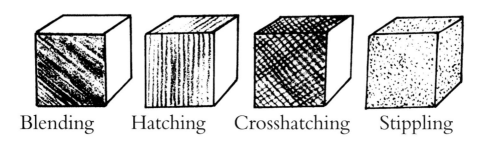

Blending   Hatching   Crosshatching   Stippling

Colored Pencil

You can blend colors with colored pencils. Color with the lighter color first. Gently color over it with the darker color until you have the effect you want.

With colored pencils, you can use the four shading techniques.

Shadows or darker values can be created by blending complementary colors.

Technique Tips

Felt-tip Pen

Felt-tip pens can be used to make either sketches or finished drawings. They are ideal for contour drawings.

Use the point of a felt-tip pen to make details.

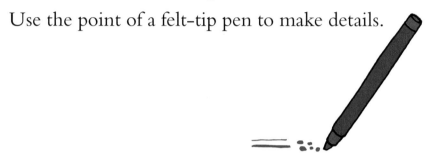

Felt-tip pens can be used for hatching, cross-hatching, and stippling.

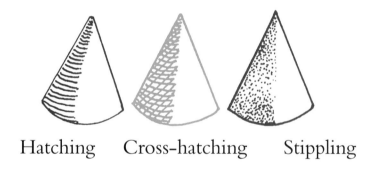

Hatching   Cross-hatching   Stippling

Always replace the cap so the felt-tip pen doesn't dry out.

Technique Tips

Marker

Markers can be used to make sketches or finished drawings. Use the point of the marker to make thin lines and small dots.

Use the side of the tip for coloring in areas and for making thick lines.

Always replace the cap so the marker doesn't dry out.

Technique Tips

Colored Chalk

Colored chalks can be used to make colorful, soft designs.

You can use the tip of the colored chalk to create lines, color shapes, and fill spaces. As with pencil, you can also use them for blending to create shadows.

Colored chalk is soft and can break easily. These pieces are still usable. Colors can be mixed or blended by smearing them together with your finger or a tissue.

Oil Pastels

Oil pastels are colors that are mixed with oil and pressed into sticks. When you press down hard with them, your pictures will look painted.

Oil pastels are soft. You can use oil pastels to color over other media, such as tempera or crayon. Then, you can scratch through this covering to create a design.

Charcoal

Charcoal is soft. It can be blended with a piece of rolled paper towel and your finger. Create dark values by coloring over an area several times. Create lighter values by erasing or coloring over the charcoal with white chalk.

Technique Tips

Tempera

1. Fill water containers halfway. Dip your brush in water. Wipe your brush on the inside edge of the container. Then, blot it on a paper towel to get rid of extra water. Stir the paints. Add a little water if a color is too thick or dry. Remember to clean your brush before using a new color.

2. Always mix colors on a palette. Put some of each color that you want to mix on the palette. Then, add the darker color a little at a time to the lighter color. Change your water when it gets too muddy.

3. To create lighter values, add white. To darken a value, add a tiny amount of black. If you have painted something too thickly, add water and blot it with a clean paper towel.

4. Use a thin, pointed brush to paint thin lines and details. For thick lines or large areas, press firmly on the tip or use a wide brush.

5. Wash your brushes when you are done. Reshape the bristles. Store brushes with the bristles up.

More About...
Technique Tips

Watercolor

1. Fill water containers halfway. Dip your brush in water. Wipe your brush on the inside edge of the container. Then, blot it on a paper towel to get rid of extra water. With your brush, add a drop of water to each watercolor cake and stir. Remember to clean your brush whenever you change colors.

2. Always mix colors on a palette. Put some of each color that you want to mix on the palette. Then, add the darker color a little at a time to the lighter color. Change your water when it gets too muddy.

3. To create lighter values, add more water. To darken a value, add a tiny amount of black.

4. Use a thin, pointed brush to paint thin lines and details. For thick lines or large areas, press firmly on the tip or use a wide brush.

5. For a softer look, tape your paper to the table with masking tape. Use a wide brush to add water to the paper, working in rows from top to bottom. This is a **wash.** Let the water soak in a little. Painting on wet paper will create a soft or fuzzy look. For sharper forms or edges, paint on dry paper, using only a little water on your brush.

6. Wash your brushes when you are done. Reshape the bristles. Store brushes with the bristles up.

Technique Tips

Printmaking: Making Stamps

Two methods for making stamps for printmaking are listed below. You can cut either a positive or negative shape into most of these objects. Be sure to talk with your teacher or another adult about what kind of tools you can use safely.

- Cut sponges into shapes.

- Draw or sculpt a design on a flat piece of modeling clay using a pencil, clay tool, tip of a paper clip, or other object.

Technique Tips

Printmaking: Printing Stamps

1. Put a small amount of water-based printing ink or some paint onto a hard, flat surface. Roll a soft roller, called a brayer, back and forth into the ink until there is an even coating of paint on both the surface and the brayer.

2. Press the stamp into the paint on the surface. The ink should cover the stamp evenly without going into the grooves of your design.

3. Or, you can coat the stamp evenly with paint using a brush. Whichever method you use, be careful not to use too much ink or paint.

4. Gently press your stamp carefully to your paper. Then, peel the paper and stamp apart and check your print. If you wish to make several prints of your design, you should ink your stamp again as needed.

5. When you have finished, wash the brayer, surface, and stamp.

More About...
Technique Tips

Collage

In a collage, objects or pieces of paper, fabric, or other materials are pasted onto a surface to create a work of art. When planning your collage, consider such things as:

- Size of shapes and spaces
- Placement of shapes and spaces
- Color schemes
- Textures

Remember that the empty (negative) spaces are also part of your design. Plan a collage as you would plan a painting or drawing. After deciding what shapes and objects you want to use, arrange them on the paper. When you have made an arrangement you like, glue your shapes and objects to the paper.

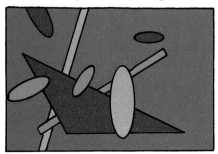

Colored Tissue Collage

When gluing colored tissue, mix a solution of one part glue to one part water.

When gluing the tissue, use an old brush to put a small amount of the glue and water solution onto the drawing paper. Next, put the tissue in place, and brush over the tissue with a small amount of the watered glue. Be careful not to get the color from the tissue on your fingers, which would create a mess. You can mix colors by overlapping different colored tissues.

Be sure to rinse your brush when you change colors. When you finish, wash the brush with soapy water.

More About...

Technique Tips

Papier-Mâché—Strip Method

The strip method of papier-mâché ("mashed paper") uses paper combined with paste. Often, papier-mâché is molded over a form that helps it keep its shape while it's drying.

1. Create a supporting form, if needed. Forms can be made from clay, wadded-up newspaper, cardboard boxes and tubes, balloons, wire, or other materials. Masking tape can be used to hold the form together.

2. Tear paper into strips. Either dip the strips into a thick mixture of paste or rub paste on the strips with your fingers. Use wide strips to cover wide forms and thin strips or small pieces to cover a small shape.

3. Apply five or six layers of strips. Lay each layer in a different direction so you can keep track of the number of strips and layers. For example, lay the first layer vertically and the second horizontally. Smooth over all rough edges with your fingers. If you are going to leave the form in place permanently, two or three layers of strips should be enough.

4. When it is dry, you can paint your sculpture.

More About...
Technique Tips

Clay

Pinch and pull clay into the desired shape.

Clay Slab Construction

To roll a slab of clay, press a ball of clay into a flat shape on a cloth-covered board. Place one 1/4" slat on each side of the clay. Use a roller to press the slab into an even thickness. With a straightened paper clip, trim the slab into the desired shape.

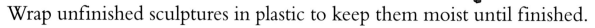

Wrap unfinished sculptures in plastic to keep them moist until finished.

When you are constructing a form, such as a container or house, with slabs of clay, it may be necessary to stuff the form with wads of newspaper to support the walls. The newspaper will burn out in the kiln.

To join two pieces of clay together:

- *score,* or scratch, both pieces so they will stick together.

- attach the pieces with some *slip,* which is watery clay.

- *squeeze* the two pieces together.

- *smooth* the edges.

204   **More About...Technique Tips**

More About...
Technique Tips

Soap and Plaster Sculpture

You can carve sculptures from clay, soap, or plaster forms. Draw the basic shape of your idea onto all sides of the form. Keep your design simple. Carve a little bit at a time, using a spoon, a paper clip, or a plastic knife, while turning your form constantly.

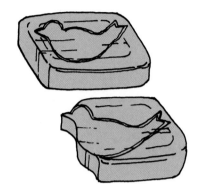

Soft Sculpture Face

Stuff a stocking or other stretchable material with polyester fill. Sew or glue on buttons, beads, sequins, fabric scraps, and other items to create facial features.

Add yarn, string, or raffia for hair. Try some of the stitches on this page to add details, such as eyebrows, wrinkles, or freckles.

You can use fabric paints for details.

Sew on a real hat, scarf, or head band. Use one of the stitches below.

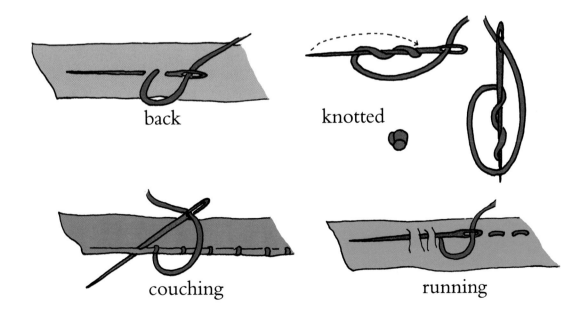

back   knotted

couching   running

More About...
Art Criticism

Frida Kahlo. (Mexican). *Frieda and Diego, Wedding Portrait*. 1931. Oil on canvas. 39 × 31 inches. San Francisco Museum of Modern Art, San Francisco, California.

DESCRIBE

List what you see in this painting. Be sure to describe the people and their clothing. Don't forget to list everything else you see.

ANALYZE

Discuss the way the artist has used line, shape, color, value, space, and texture.

What kind of balance has the artist used?

Can you find examples of rhythm, variety, and harmony?

Has the artist used emphasis to make us notice one thing more than others?

Frida Kahlo. (Mexican). *Frieda and Diego, Wedding Portrait.* 1931. Oil on canvas. 39 × 31 inches. San Francisco Museum of Modern Art, San Francisco, California.

More About...
Art Criticism

INTERPRET

What is happening? What is the artist telling us about these two people? What can you tell about their relationship?

DECIDE

Have you ever seen another work of art that looks like this painting?

Is this painting successful because it is realistic? Is it successful because it is well-organized? Is it successful because you have strong feelings when you study it?

LOOK

Frida Kahlo. (Mexican). *Frieda and Diego, Wedding Portrait.*
1931. Oil on canvas. 39 × 31 inches. San Francisco
Museum of Modern Art, San Francisco, California.

LOOK AGAIN

Look at the work of art.

What happened just before and just after in this work of art?

What sounds, smells, or feelings are in this work of art?

What kind of music would be playing in this work of art?

If you could take away from or add images or elements to the work of art, what would they be and why?

Is there a relationship between the work of art and your experiences?

LOOK INSIDE

Look at the work of art.

Imagine you are one of these people. Who are you? What are you thinking? How do you feel?

If you could add yourself to the painting, what would you look like? What would you be doing?

Act out or tell the story in the work of art with a beginning, a middle, and an end.

Draw what you can't see in this work of art. Are there hidden images that should be revealed?

Select or create one symbol of your own that you believe represents your impression of this work of art.

Frida Kahlo. (Mexican). *Frieda and Diego, Wedding Portrait*. 1931. Oil on canvas. 39 × 31 inches. San Francisco Museum of Modern Art, San Francisco, California.

LOOK OUTSIDE

Look at the work of art.

How is this like or different from your own world?

How would you change this work of art to be more like your world? What would the changes be? What would the artwork look like?

What does the artist want you to know or think about in this work of art?

Describe your journey about viewing this work of art. Include your thoughts, ideas, and changes in thinking.

If you could ask the work of art questions about itself, what would you ask?

How have you been changed by examining this work of art?

What will you remember about this work?

Artist unknown.
Adena Effigy Figure.
1000–300 B.C. United States.

Artist unknown.
Three Cows and One Horse.
15,000–13,000 B.C. France.

Artist unknown.
Statues from Abu Temple.
2700–2000 B.C. Iraq.

Artist unknown.
Tutankhamen Mask (side view).
c. 1340 B.C. Egypt.

Artist unknown.
Chuang.
1100 B.C. China.

Artist unknown.
Colossal Head.
1500–300 B.C. Mexico.

Artist unknown.
Woman Playing Harp.
(Detail from vase.) c. 490 B.C.

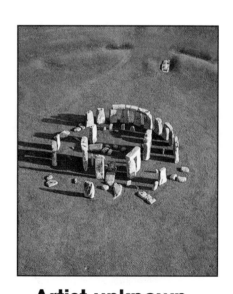

Artist unknown.
Parthenon.
448–432 B.C. Greece.

Artist unknown.
Stonehenge.
1800–1400 B.C. England.

More About...Art History

Artist unknown.
Shiva as Lord of the Dance.
1000. India.

Artist unknown.
Ravenna Apse Mosaic. (Detail).
A.D. 100. Italy.

Artist unknown.
The Pantheon.
A.D. 118–125. Italy.

Artist unknown.
Hagia Sophia.
A.D. 532–537. Turkey.

Artist unknown.
The Great Stupa (at Sanchi).
200–100 B.C. India.

Artist unknown.
Page from *The Book of Lindisfarne*.
Late 600s. England.

Artist unknown.
*Pagoda of the Temple
of the Six Banyan Trees.*
A.D. 537. China.

Artist unknown.
Stupa (at Borobudur).
800. Indonesia.

Artist unknown.
Great Mosque
(at Samarra).
648–852. Iraq.

Rembrandt van Rijn.
Self-Portrait.
1660. The Netherlands.

Leonardo da Vinci.
Mona Lisa.
1503–1505. Italy.

Artist unknown.
Bayon Temple at Angkor Thom.
1100s–1200s. Cambodia.

Artist unknown.
Shrine Head. (Yorub).
1100–1300. Nigeria.

Torii Kiyotada.
Actor of the Ichikawa Clan.
1710–1740. Japan.

Artist unknown.
Chartres Cathedral.
1145–1220. France.

Thomas Jefferson.
Monticello.
1770–1784. United States.

Artist unknown.
Bayeux Tapestry. (Detail).
1070–1080. England.

Artist unknown.
Taj Mahal.
1632–1648. India.

Artist unknown.
Anasazi culture petroglyphs.
United States.

More About...Art History   **219**

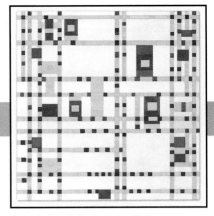

Piet Mondrian.
Broadway Boogie-Woogie.
1941. The Netherlands.

Claude Monet.
Impression, Sunrise.
1872. France.

Edgar Degas.
Little Dancer of Fourteen.
1880–1881. France.

Katsushika Hokusai.
The Great Wave off Kanagawa.
1831–1833. Japan.

Pablo Picasso.
Gertrude Stein.
1906. Spain.

Chuck Close.
Self-Portrait.
1987. United States.

Jackson Pollock.
Convergence.
1952. United States.

Maria Martínez.
Black on Black Pot.
1920. United States.

Alexander Calder.
Untitled Mobile.
1959. United States.

More About...
Subject Matter

A rtists create art about many topics. *Subject matter* is the artist's term for the content of artwork. For example, the subject of a painting can be a simple portrait. The subject might be an everyday experience like bike riding. These kinds of subject matter are easy to identify. But subject matter becomes more difficult to understand when the artwork stands for something beyond itself. Look at these artworks and become familiar with the different terms used for subject matter.

Portrait

Gerard Dou. (Dutch). *Self-Portrait.* Oil on wood. $19\frac{1}{4} \times 15\frac{3}{8}$ inches. The Metropolitan Museum of Art, New York, New York. Bequest of Benjamin Altman, 1913.

More About...
Subject Matter

Seascape

Winslow Homer. *Gulf Stream.* 1899.
Oil on canvas. $28\frac{1}{8} \times 49\frac{1}{8}$ inches. The
Metropolitan Museum of Art, New York,
New York. Catherine Lorillard Wolfe
Collection, Wolfe Fund, 1906.

Subject Matter

Allegory

Jan van Eyck. (Flemish). *Portrait of Giovanni Arnolfini and His Wife Giovanna Cenami.* 1434. Oil on wood panel. 32 × 23½ inches. Courtesy of the Trustees of the National Gallery, London, England. Bridgeman/Art Resource, NY.

Still Life

Vincent van Gogh. (Dutch). *Sunflowers.* 1887. Oil on canvas.
17 × 24 inches. Metropolitan Museum of Art, New York.

Subject Matter

Genre

Carmen Lomas Garza.
(American). *Cakewalk.*
1987. Acrylics.
36 × 48 inches. Collection
of Paula Maciel-Beneke and
Norbert Beneke.
Soquel, California.
Photo by M. Lee Fatherree.

Nonobjective

Piet Mondrian. (Dutch). *Broadway
Boogie-Woogie.* 1942–43. Oil on
canvas. 50 × 50 inches. The
Museum of Modern Art, New York.
Given anonymously. Photograph
©1998 The Museum of Modern
Art, New York.

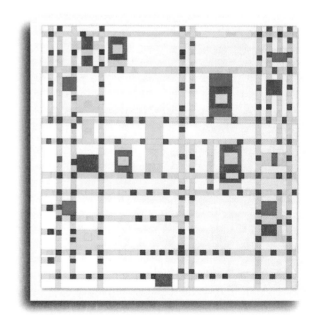

Symbolic

Artist unknown. (United States). *Buckskin Ghost Dance Arapaho Dress.* Philadelphia Museum of Art, Philadelphia, Pennsylvania. Photo by Graydon Wood, 1994.

More About...
Still-Life Drawing

Everything you see is filled with lines and shapes you already know how to draw.

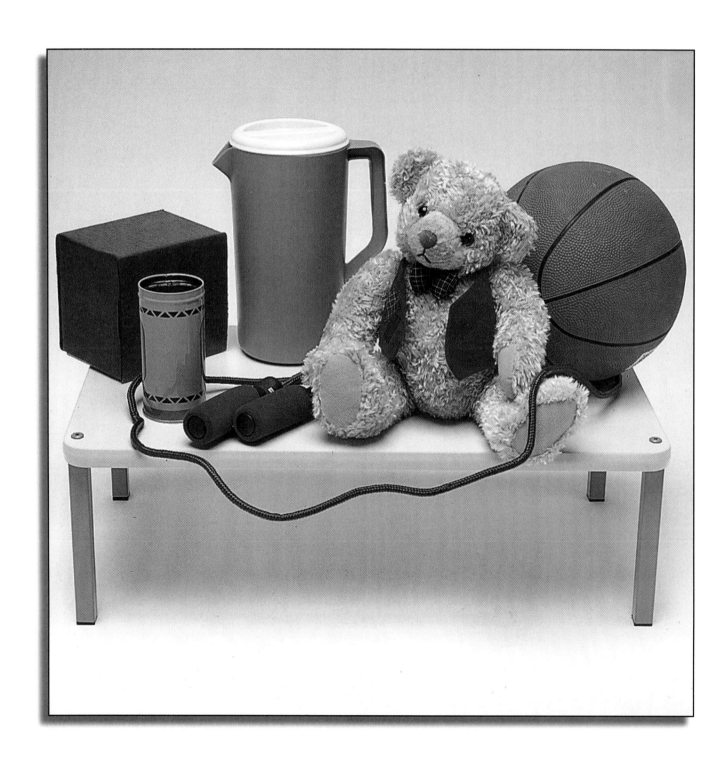

More About...
Still-Life Drawing

LOOK

Look at the photograph of the still life.

✓ Find the horizontal lines on the edge of the table.

✓ Find the vertical lines on the sides of the red box.

✓ Find the diagonal lines on the top and bottom edges of the red box. Because you see three sides of the box at once, you can tell that it is a form.

✓ The top of the can is an ellipse, not a circle or a straight line. An ellipse is a flattened circle with rounded ends. The curved line of an ellipse narrows at the ends. It does not have points. Find another ellipse in the photo. Find an ellipse in your room.

✓ Find the can in the photograph. Its form is a cylinder. Its top is an ellipse. Its sides are vertical lines. Its bottom is a curved line. The curve of the bottom is almost the same as the lower curve of the ellipse at the top.

PRACTICE

Practice drawing cylinders. First draw an ellipse. Next, draw a vertical line down from each end of the ellipse. Draw the bottom of the cylinder by connecting the ends of the vertical lines with a curved line similar to the lower curve in the ellipse.

More About...
Drawing People

People are made of free-form shapes. These shapes change depending upon what position a person is in.

More About...
Drawing People

LOOK

Look at the three people in the photograph. Notice the shape and size of the heads, necks, torsos, arms, legs, hands, and feet. These are free-form shapes.

- ✓ How is the shape of the person's head that's sitting sideways different from the head of a person who is facing you? The person's head facing you is like an oval. Actually, it is a picture of an oval-shaped form.

- ✓ The person's head facing sideways is a picture of a free-form form. The bodies are also pictures of free-form forms.

- ✓ Look at the people in your room. You are looking at free-form forms.

- ✓ Notice how the form of a person's body changes if he or she is sitting, standing facing you, or standing sideways. When a person is facing you, the body appears wider than when standing sideways.

- ✓ Look at the horizontal stripes on the shirts of the people in the photograph. Notice how they curve around the bodies and arms. This shows their form. You can draw curved lines across parts of a person's body to show his or her rounded thickness.

PRACTICE

Look at the people in your classroom. Practice drawing people. Draw curved lines across parts of their bodies to show their form.

More About...
Drawing Landscapes

When you look at a landscape, you can see that some things are in front of or behind other things.

More About...
Drawing Landscapes

LOOK

Look at the landscape with the cows.

- ☑ Look at the cow in the **foreground,** the front of the picture.
- ☑ Look at the cow in the **background,** the back of the picture.
- ☑ The area between the foreground and background is the **middle ground.** It is in the center of the paper. Find the cows in the middle ground. They look smaller than the cow in the foreground. They appear larger than the cow in the background.

The difference in the appearance of the cows' sizes gives the picture depth. The cow in the foreground is larger because it is closer.

You can also see more detail in the foreground. Look for the individual blades of grass at the bottom of the picture. Can you see the eyes of the cow in the foreground?

Look at the objects in the middle ground and the background. How have the details changed? Things that are farther away have less detail.

PRACTICE

Practice drawing an object in your classroom such as a pencil, a book, or something you like. Look at the lines that outline the edges and ridges of the object. Draw them.

Now study the lines that make the details on the object. Draw them.

Artist unknown
*Ipuy and his Wife
Receiving Offerings
from Their Children*
1275 B.C.
page 63

**Domenico
Ghirlandaio**
*Francesco Sasetti
and His Son Teodoro*
c. 1480
page 110

Artist unknown
Mask
12th–9th century B.C.
page 123

Raphael
Bindo Altoviti
c. 1515
page 114

Artist unknown
*Featherwork
Neckpiece*
1350–1476
page 54

Artist unknown
Ardabil Carpet
1540
page 144

Artist unknown
*Deep Dish/Spain/
from Valencia*
1430
page 145

**Sofonisba
Anguissola**
*The Sisters of the
Artist and Their
Governess*
1555
page 141

Visual Index

Nanha the Mughal
Emperor Shah Jahan and His Son, Suja
1625–30
page 111

Francisco Goya
Don Manuel Osorio Manrique de Zuniga
1784
page 107

Jean-Étienne Liotard
A Frankish Woman and Her Servant
1750
page 67

Artist unknown
Dead-man Mask
Nineteenth century
page 122

Giovanni Pannini
Interior of St. Peters, Rome
1754
page 152

Artist unknown
Navajo Loom with Wool Blanket
Nineteenth century
page 170

Hubert Robert
The Artist Drawing a Young Girl
1773
page 106

Artist unknown
Blouse
Nineteenth century
page 167

Visual Index

Edward Hicks
Cornell Farm
1848
page 153

Vincent van Gogh
A Pair of Boots
1887
page 66

Claude Monet
The Arrival of the Normandy Train at the Gare Saint-Lazare
1877
page 148

William M. Chase
The Park
1888
page 182

Auguste Renoir
Marguerite (Margot) Bérard
1879
page 115

Artist unknown
Navajo Blanket Eye Dazzler
1890
page 51

James Tissot
Women of Paris: The Circus Lover
1883–1885
page 140

Auguste Renoir
Two Young Girls at the Piano
1892
page 33

Visual Index

Artist unknown
Kwele Face Mask
19th–20th century
page 123

Artist unknown
Caravan
(End View)
1915
page 85

Käthe Kollwitz
The Downtrodden
1900
page 29

Amedeo Modigliani
*Portrait of a Polish
Woman*
1918
page 119

Arthur Lismer
*The Guide's Home
Algonquin*
1914
page 149

M. C. Escher
Sky and Water
c. 1920
page 80

Artist unknown
Caravan
(Outside View)
1915
page 84

Edward Hopper
House by the Railroad
1925
page 156

Visual Index

Ralph Steiner
American Rural Baroque
1930
page 37

Diego Rivera
Dance in Tehuantepec
ca 1935
page 32

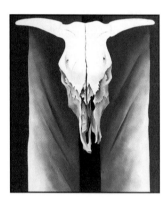

Georgia O'Keeffe
Cow's Skull: Red, White, and Blue
1931
page 136

Frank Lloyd Wright
Fallingwater
1936–1939
page 93

Diego Rivera
Detroit Industry (Mural)—South Wall
1932–1933
page 179

Elon Webster
False Face Mask
1937
page 122

Charles Sheeler
American Interior
1934
page 157

Georgia O'Keeffe
Red and Pink Rocks and Teeth
1938
page 50

Visual Index

Joan Miró
The Beautiful Bird Revealing the Unknown to a Pair of Lovers
1941
page 20

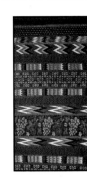

Artist unknown
Maya/Huipil (detail)
plate 263
c. 1950
page 16

M. C. Escher
Reptiles
1943
page 81

Robert McCall
Space Station #1
c. 1950
page 89

Charles Sheeler
Incantation
1946
page 17

Le Corbusier
Chapelle de Notre-Dame du Haut
1950–1955
page 96

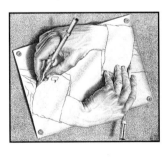

M. C. Escher
Drawing Hands
1948
page 24

Jørn Oberg Utzon
Opera House
1957
page 97

Visual Index

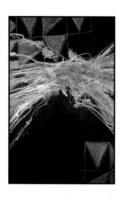

Willis Bing Davis
*Ancestral Spirit
Dance Series*
c. 1960
page 55

Jerome Liebling
*Young Boy,
Minneapolis*
1964
page 36

Manabu Mabe
*Melancholy
Metropolis*
1961
page 59

Romare Bearden
She Ba
1970
page 175

Jasper Johns
Map
1962
page 47

Elizabeth Catlett
Sharecropper
1970
page 28

Fernando Botero
Ruben's Wife
1963
page 118

Jasper Johns
Cups 4 Picasso
1972
page 76

Visual Index

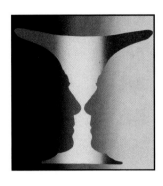

Jasper Johns
Cups 4 Picasso
1972
page 77

Elizabeth Plater-Zyberk
Seaside, Florida, Walkway
1980s
page 92

George Segal
Walk Don't Walk
1976
page 126

Duane Hanson
Football Player
1981
page 127

Tommye Scanlin
Crow, Crow
c. 1980
page 171

Wendy Fay Dixon
Deidre
1982
page 25

Ben Jones
King Family
1980
page 46

Paul Wonner
Dutch Still Life with Art Books and Field Guide to Western Birds
1982
page 21

Visual Index

Janet Fish
After Leslie Left
1983–1984
page 174

Chuck Close
Self Portrait
1987
page 137

Robert Lostutter
Baird Trogon
1985
page 58

John Biggers
Tree House
1990–1992
page 178

George McNeil
Deliverance Disco
c. 1987
page 62

Anne Beard
Rodeo Jacket
Late twentieth
century
page 166

Roger Brown
*Homesick Proof
Space Station*
1987
page 88

Artist unknown
Playground
1990s
page 183

Visual Index

Glossary

Pronunciation Key

at; **ā**pe; f**ä**r; c**â**re; **e**nd; m**ē**; **i**t; **ī**ce; p**î**erce; h**o**t; **ō**ld; s**ô**ng, f**ô**rk; **oi**l; **ou**t; **u**p; **ū**se; r**ü**le; p**ú**ll; t**û**rn; **ch**in; si**ng**; **sh**op; **th**in; **th**is; **hw** in **wh**ite; **zh** in trea**s**ure. The symbol ə stands for the unstressed vowel sound in **a**bout, tak**e**n, penc**i**l, lem**o**n, and circ**u**s.

alternate rhythm
(ôl´ tər nit ri<u>th</u>´ əm), **noun**

When one motif is repeated after a second, different motif.

analogous color scheme
(ə nal´ ə gəs kul´ ər skēm´), **noun**

A color scheme using colors that are side by side on the color wheel.

analogous colors
(ə nal´ ə gəs kul´ ərz), **noun**

Colors that are side by side on the color wheel.

appliqué
(ap´ li kā´), **noun**

Art made by attaching fabric shapes onto a fabric background by gluing or sewing.

architect
(är´ kə tekt), **noun**

A person who plans and designs buildings, cities, and bridges.

architecture
(är´ ki tek´ chər), **noun**

The art of designing and planning the construction of buildings, cities, and bridges.

armature
(är´ mə chər), **noun**

A framework for supporting material used in sculpting.

assemblage
(ä säm bläzh´), **noun**

A work of art in which a variety of objects are assembled to create one complete piece.

asymmetry
(ā sim´ i trē), **noun**

Another name for *informal balance.* Asymmetry is a way of organizing parts of a design so that unlike objects have equal visual weight.

balance
(bal´ əns), **noun**

The principle of design that deals with visual weight in a work of art.

body proportions
(bod´ ē prə pôr shənz), **noun**

Ratios of one part of the body to another.

Glossary

central axis
(sen´ trəl   ak´ sis), **noun**

The central dividing line, sometimes imaginary.

color intensity
(kul´ ər   in ten´ si tē), **noun**

The brightness or dullness of a color.

color scheme
(kul´ ər   skēm´), **noun**

A plan for organizing colors.

complementary colors
(kom´ plə men tə rē   kul´ ərz), **noun**

Colors that are opposite each other on the color wheel.

complex geometric shapes
(kom´ pleks   jē´ ə met´ rik shāps), **noun**

Shapes created from a combination of geometric shapes.

contrast
(kon´ trast), **noun (verb)**

A difference created when elements are placed next to each other in a work of art.

cool color
(kül´   kul´ ər), **noun**

A color that seems to move away from the viewer and suggests coolness. Green, blue, and violet are cool colors.

cross-hatching
(krôs´ hach´ ing), **noun**

A shading technique in which two or more sets of parallel lines cross each other.

curved
(kûrvd), **adj.**

A line that bends and changes direction slowly.

depth
(depth), **noun**

The appearance of distance on a flat surface.

diagonal
(dī ag ə nəl), **noun (adj.)**

A slanted line.

direct observation
(di rekt´ ob zər vā shən), **noun**

The technique of artists studying an object from various viewpoints, looking closely at the important details and recording those details in their drawings.

distortion
(di stôr´ shən), **noun**

Changing an object or figure out of normal shape to communicate ideas or feelings.

emphasis
(em´ fə sis), **noun**

The principle of design that stresses one area in a work of art.

Glossary

exaggeration
(eg zaj´ ə rā´ shən), **noun**

Increasing or enlarging an object or a figure or one of its parts to communicate ideas or feelings.

facial proportions
(fā´ shəl prə pôr shənz), **noun**

The relationship of one feature of a face to another feature.

flowing rhythm
(flō´ ing ri<u>th</u>´ əm), **noun**

Rhythm that repeats wavy lines.

focal point
(fo´ kəl point´), **noun**

The area of an artwork that is emphasized.

form
(fôrm), **noun**

Any object that can be measured in three ways: length, width, and depth.

formal balance
(fôr´ məl bal´ əns), **noun**

When equal, or very similar, elements are placed on opposite sides of a central line.

free-form shapes
(frē´ fôrm´ shāps), **noun**

Uneven, irregular shapes made with curved lines, straight lines, or a combination of the two.

geometric shapes
(jē´ ə met´ rik shāps), **noun**

Shapes that can be described by mathematical formulas, such as a circle, a square, a triangle, or a rectangle.

gradation
(grād ā´ shən), **noun**

A gradual change of one value to another.

harmony
(här´ mə nē), **noun**

Concerned with similarities of separate but related parts.

hatching
(hach´ ing), **noun**

A shading technique using a series of fine repeated parallel lines.

highlights
(hī´ līts´), **noun**

Small areas of white or light values.

horizon line
(hə rī´ zən līn´), **noun**

The point at which Earth and sky meet.

horizontal
(hôr´ ə zon´ təl), **adj. (noun)**

A line that moves from side to side.

Glossary

hue
(hū), **noun**

Another word for *color*.

imitated texture
(im´ i tā təd   teks´ chər), **noun**

A two-dimensional texture that imitates or simulates a real texture.

informal balance
(in fôr´ məl   bal´ əns), **noun**

A way of organizing parts of a design so that unlike objects have equal visual weight.

intermediate hues
(in´ tər´ mē dē it   hūz´), **noun**

Made by mixing a primary hue with a secondary hue.

isolation
(ī´ sə lā´ shən), **noun**

When an object is placed alone and away from all the other objects in an artwork.

linear perspective
(lin ē´ ər   pər spek´ tiv), **noun**

A way of using lines to show distance and depth.

line
(līn), **noun**

A mark drawn by a tool such as a pencil, pen, or paintbrush as it moves across a surface.

location
(lō cā´ shən), **noun**

When the eyes are naturally drawn toward the center of an artwork.

mandala
(man´ də lə), **noun**

A radial design divided into sections or wedges, each of which contains an image.

matte
(mat), **adj.**

Textured surfaces that reflect a soft light, with an almost dull look.

monochromatic
(mon´ ə krō mat´ ik), **adj.**

One color plus all the tints and shades of that color.

monochromatic color scheme
(mon´ ə krō mat´ ik   kul´ ər skēm´), **noun**

A color scheme using one color plus all the tints and shades of that color.

motif
(mō tēf´), **noun**

The object or group of objects that is repeated.

negative space
(neg´ ə tiv   spās´), **noun**

The empty space that surrounds objects, shapes, and forms.

Glossary

nonobjective painting
(non´ əb jek´ tiv pān´ ting),
noun

It contains shapes, lines, and colors, not objects or people.

one-point perspective
(wun´ point´ pər spek´ tiv),
noun

One way of using lines to show distance and depth, with all lines that move back into space meeting at one point.

pattern
(pat´ ərn), **noun**

The use of shapes, colors, or lines repeated in a planned way; describes visual rhythm.

perception
(pər sep´ shən), **noun**

The act of looking at something carefully and thinking deeply about what is seen.

perspective
(pər spek´ tiv), **noun**

The method used to create the illusion of depth on a flat surface.

point of view
(point´ əv vū´), **noun**

The position from which the viewer looks at an object.

positive space
(poz´ i tiv spās´), **noun**

Refers to any object, shape, or form in a work of art.

primary hues
(prī´ mer ē hūz´), **noun**

Red, blue, and yellow.

profile proportions
(prō´ fīl prə pôr´ shənz), **noun**

The relationship of one feature of a face to another feature when looking from the side view.

progressive
(prə gres´ iv), **adj.**

Changing or moving forward.

progressive reversal
(prə gres´ iv ri vûr səl), **noun**

When an object starts out as one object or form and slowly changes into another object or form.

progressive rhythm
(prə gres´ iv ri<u>th</u>´ əm), **noun**

When a motif changes each time it is repeated.

proportion
(prə pôr´ shən), **noun**

The principle of art concerned with the size relationships of one part to another.

Glossary

radial balance
(rā´ dē əl   bal´ əns), **noun**

When the elements of design (line, shape, color, and form) seem to radiate or come out from a center point.

random rhythm
(ran´ dəm   ri<u>th</u>´ əm), **noun**

When a motif is repeated in no apparent order.

ratio
(rā´ shē ō´), **noun**

A comparison of size between two things.

realistic scale
(rē´ ə lis´ tik   skāl), **noun**

In a work of art where everything seems to fit together and make sense in size relationships.

regular rhythm
(reg´ yə lər   ri<u>th</u>´ əm), **noun**

Identical motifs repeated with equal amounts of space between them.

relief print
(ri lēf´   print), **noun**

A technique in which the design to be printed is raised from the background.

rough
(ruf), **adj.**

Textured surfaces that reflect the light unevenly.

scale
(skāl), **noun**

Size as measured against a standard reference.

secondary hues
(sek´ ən der´ ē   hūz´), **noun**

The result of mixing two primary hues.

shade
(shād), **noun**

Any dark value of a hue.

shading
(shā´ ding), **noun**

A technique for darkening values by adding black or darkening an area by repeating several lines close together.

shadows
(shad´ ōz), **noun**

Shaded, or darker, areas in a drawing or painting.

shape
(shāp), **noun**

Two-dimensional figure that can be measured in two ways: length and height.

Glossary

shape reversal
(shāp′ ri vûr′ səl), **noun**

When a shape or positive space starts out as one image and then in another image becomes the negative space.

shiny
(shī′ nē), **adj.**

Textured surfaces that reflect a bright light.

smooth
(smü<u>th</u>), **adj.**

Textured surfaces that reflect the light evenly.

space
(spās), **noun**

The element of art that refers to the area between, around, above, below, and within objects.

stippling
(stip′ ling), **noun**

A shading technique using dots. The closer the dots, the darker the area.

symmetry
(sim′ i trē), **noun**

A type of formal balance when two sides are mirror images of each other.

tactile texture
(tak′ təl teks′ chər), **noun**

Actual texture that you can touch and feel.

tessellation
(te′ se lā′ shen), **noun**

A type of shape reversal that changes quickly and fits together like a puzzle.

texture
(teks′ chər), **noun**

The element of art that refers to how things feel, or look as if they might feel if touched.

three-dimensional form
(thrē′ di men′ shə nəl fôrm′), **noun**

Anything that can be measured by height, width, and depth.

tint
(tint), **noun**

Any light value of a hue.

two-dimensional shape
(tü′ di men′ shə nəl shāp′), **noun**

Flat figures, measured by length and width.

unity
(ū′ ni tē), **noun**

The quality of wholeness or oneness that is achieved by properly using the elements and principles of art.

unrealistic scale
(un′ rē ə lis′ tik skāl′), **noun**

When size relationships do not make sense in a work of art.

Glossary

value
(val´ ū), **noun**

Lightness or darkness of a color or object.

vanishing point
(van´ i shing   point´), **noun**

The point on the horizon line where all the lines moving back into a space seem to meet.

variety
(və rī´ ə tē), **noun**

The principle of design concerned with difference or contrast. Variety is the opposite of harmony.

vertical line
(vûr´ tə kəl   līn), **noun**

A line that moves up and down.

visual movement
(vizh´ ü əl   müv´ mənt), **noun**

Creating the illusion of movement through visual rhythm.

visual rhythm
(vizh´ ü əl   ri<u>th</u>´ əm), **noun**

Rhythm created by the repetition of shapes, colors, or lines.

visual texture
(vizh´ ü əl   teks´ chər), **noun**

The way something looks like it might feel if you could touch it.

warm color
(wôrm´   kul´ ər), **noun**

Color that seems to move toward the viewer and suggests warmth and energy. Red, orange, and yellow are warm colors.

warp threads
(wôrp´   thredz´), **noun**

Vertical threads attached to a loom.

weft threads
(weft´   thredz´), **noun**

Threads that are woven over and under the warp threads.

zigzag
(zig´ zag´), **noun (adj.)**

Diagonal lines that connect and change direction sharply.

Index

Index

Index

Index

Index